The Whole Earth Textbook:

A Survival Manual for Students

WILLIAM H. PIVAR

**College of the Desert
Palm Desert, California**

1978

W. B. SAUNDERS COMPANY • Philadelphia • London • Toronto

W. B. Saunders Company: West Washington Square
Philadelphia, Pa. 19105

1 St. Anne's Road
Eastbourne, East Sussex BN21 3UN, England

1 Goldthorne Avenue
Toronto, Ontario M8Z 5T9, Canada

Library of Congress Cataloging in Publication Data

Pivar, William H
   The whole earth textbook.

   1. College student orientation. 2. Study, Method of. 3. Report
writing. 4. College costs. 5. College students—Employment. I. Title.
LB2343.3.P54   378.1'98   77-11350
ISBN 0-7216-7250-7

Photographs by Corinne E. Pivar

The Whole Earth Textbook: A Survival Manual for Students   ISBN   0-7216-7250-7

Last digit is the print number: 9   8   7   6   5   4   3   2   1

Acknowledgments

I would like to thank the following people for their help in the preparation of this book: Douglas Garrison, Associate Professor of English at College of the Desert, whose proof-readings were invaluable; Amy Shapiro, the patient copy editor whose guidance helped me through the final days of writing; Rod Fuss and Pat Connelly, of the Lakeland Council on Alcoholism and Other Drug Abuse, for sharing their knowledge and experience; the reviewers, whose constructive criticism helped to keep the book on the right track; and Corinne Pivar, my wife and photographer for this text, without whose help this book would never have been written.

Contents

CHAPTER 10

EMPLOYMENT DURING AND AFTER COLLEGE...113

APPENDIX

Introduction

As a reasonable person, you wouldn't consider driving across the country without a road map. You would want to study the map and consider the various alternative routes. You would then choose a route that you considered best for your needs.

At the present time you are poised, ready to start on a different type of journey. The path that you will take through college will directly affect every day of the rest of your life.

This book is more than just your road map to college. It will serve as an aid to you in selecting a destination or career goal. It will help you to explore and choose from the various routes you can take to arrive at your career goal.

This book provides you with the survival skills necessary for your successful journey through college. It prepares you for what lies ahead.

On any long trip you are liable to run into the unexpected, such as: detours, road construction, slowdowns, or even mechanical difficulties. In the same manner, you may encounter unexpected situations in college. This book will help you in your decision-making regarding the problems that may arise.

This book is your starting point for college. It is a source book for college information. Use it as a reference and a tool.

You should keep in mind that no book can tell you what is best for you. The personal decisions of your life should be made by you alone. However, this book will help prepare you to make informed personal decisions.

We wish you good luck on your journey.

The Whole Earth Textbook

A Survival Manual for Students

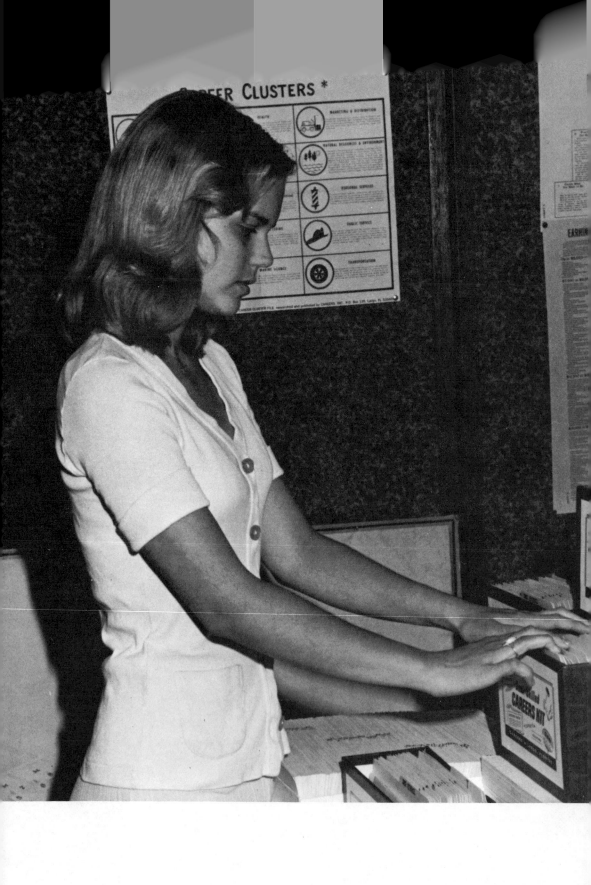

Chapter 1
Self Analysis

Starting college or even just planning for college probably leaves you with mixed feelings. While you have looked forward to college, you are leaving a familiar routine and now must give serious thought to your future. Probably everyone just starting college has asked himself, "What now? Where do I go from here?" You want to know what the future holds for you, and you want success.

Just dreaming about your future is not enough. Many students finish college with no real plans, and the first job they get tends to determine the direction of their entire working career, a period that may exceed 40 years.

Often students spend less time in analyzing their career needs than they spend in buying a car. When they buy a car, they consider the qualities they want in a car and their priorities. These might be price, fuel economy, condition, age, performance, maintenance, style, capacity, etc. After weighing these factors and considering their priorities, they make an informed decision based on their own particular needs.

In the same manner as you buy a car you can plan your future. You can analyze your individual needs and choose a career that satisfies those needs. It is possible to make an informed decision about what direction your career takes. You can control where you are going from here. A career is too important to leave to chance and also too important to be decided by parents, friends, or relatives. Your career choice must be your own and must be directed by your own specific needs.

Certainly there is more to life than just finishing college and getting a job. Nevertheless, a great deal of your life is going to revolve around your career. If you can do a job well, you are going to have self pride, and if you are proud of the work you are doing, you can expect to be happy in your work and in your life. That is what success is really all about.

If you are completely lost and have no idea where you want to go, I suggest you obtain occupational aptitude testing. The General Aptitude Test Battery (GATB) is available from many YMCAs, state employment services, welfare offices, etc. Your college guidance center can either give you the test or tell you where in your area it can be taken. It can usually be obtained without charge.

There are other tests available, such as the STRONG test, which indicates vocational interest; the Kuder Test, which shows interest preference; and the 16 PF Test, which tests your personality. Testing will show natural ability, areas of interest, and personality factors. However, no test has been developed that will accurately decide the best career choice for you. You should use the tests as guides to areas of interest that deserve further consideration. They can provide a starting point for you to work from.

There are over 30,000 different types of jobs. Many jobs that on the surface appear very different actually are similar. That is, the same skills and training required for one might prepare you for others. This is important, since you should realize that even after graduation you are not necessarily locked into a single career. You will find that many alternative careers are available that utilize much of the same training.

Older students who start college years after completing high school generally have much more specific educational and career goals in mind than students who enter college directly from high school. For these older students, experiences have influenced their goal decisions and have motivated them to further their education. Goals of older students are sometimes well suited to the individual based on interest, talent, and needs. However, although the goals are specific, often they were not really analyzed with the individual's needs in mind. Career guidance can reinforce, modify, or completely redirect present goals. Career guidance isn't just for those who have not made up their minds. It is a worthwhile process for everyone.

The first step in career guidance is product evaluation. In this case the product is you. Salespeople who have to market products know that to be successful they must have product knowledge. They must know both the strengths and weaknesses of the products and how they can be utilized.

You can perform your own self analysis. By answering the following questions in the personal inventory you can determine areas of interest that should be explored further.

1. What skills and special training do I now possess? **PERSONAL INVENTORY**

With this question we reveal present skills, which might complement your educational training.
2. What do I consider to be my greatest assets?

3. A future employer would consider my greatest assets to be:
(If you are currently employed, answer this question as to your present employer.)

You should ask yourself, "How do these assets fit into my career plan?" Any career choice should make use of your personal assets. Your career choice should be geared to you.
4. What are my weaknesses?

5. An employer would consider my greatest weakness to be:

There are two solutions to areas of weakness. One is to strengthen yourself in these areas with additional training.

The other would be a career choice that does not rely on areas you consider to be weaknesses.

6.   What have I done in the past that I am really proud of?

7.   Why?

8.   What have I done that I would like to do again?

9.   What work have I done in the past that I really enjoyed?

10.   What specifically was there about this work that appealed to me?

11.   What are my favorite hobbies?

12. What type of work is there that would be more fun than work to me?

13. What types of jobs do I feel would not become boring to me?

These questions are career pointers. If you can come up with a career choice that gives you pride, that you enjoy, and that stimulates you, your chances of having a happy and successful career are greatly enhanced.

14. What natural mechanical ability do I have?

15. At high school, in what subjects did I get the best grades?

16. What subjects took the least effort on my part?

These questions are also career pointers. They relate to natural ability as well as interest.

17. Who do I know who has the kind of job I would like to have?

18. What specifically is there about these jobs that I like?

These are specific career pointers. However, when you analyze what these jobs entail they may not be as attractive as they initially seem.

19. What work have I done in the past that I have not liked . . . and why?

20. What career areas am I definitely not interested in?

21. Why?

These questions point out problem areas. Students often refuse to consider an entire career field even though it is only one aspect of the career they dislike. Frequently the reason for not considering a career is a lack of understanding of what the career actually entails.

22. What skills or training do I wish I had?

23. Why?

These again are pointers to your own special interests.

24. How would I rate my verbal communication ability?

25. How would I rate my written communication ability?

Possession of good skills in these areas is important in most administrative positions. Verbal skills are very important in people-oriented positions such as sales or teaching.

26. Do I want to help people?

27. How?

These questions open up for consideration the field of public service. Actually this includes many service and professional jobs.

28. Do I prefer to deal with people or things?

If you are an introvert you would probably prefer work you can do by yourself. Some administrative and professional jobs, as well as many mechanically-oriented positions, fall in this category. If you enjoy people you should consider jobs requiring public contact or team effort.

29. Do I enjoy travel?

30. Do I enjoy driving?

These questions will help you to determine whether you should make a career choice that would require a great deal of travel.

31. Would I prefer office work or outside work?

32. Would I prefer to have my day planned for me, or would I prefer to do my own planning and goal setting?

33. Would I prefer regular working hours?

34. Are the number of hours I work of major importance to me?

35. Do I want to be my own boss?

These questions reveal interests and attitudes that can significantly limit areas of career choice.

36.   What, if any, are my physical limitations?

Physical limitations can eliminate some careers requiring unusual stamina or pressure.

37.   Must I remain in the present geographical area?

38.   Where would I be willing to move?

39.   Where would I not move?

If you must remain in an area or are either unwilling to relocate or will relocate only in particular areas, you are eliminating many specific careers from your consideration. (They do not need many oceanographers in Denver.)

40.   How important is job security to me?

If security is of prime consideration to you, you probably would not want to plan to go into business for yourself. In your career choice you might want to trade off some degree of job satisfaction for greater security.

41.   Am I ambitious?

If advancement is important to you, and you would not be content to remain in a mid-management position, you should give consideration to postgraduate work if it is applicable.

42.   Prior to answering these questions my career goal was:

43.   I am suited for this career because:

You are now in a much better position to analyze what was and may still be your career goal.

44.   What are my social and economic aspirations?

45.   Is my career goal compatible with my social and economic goals?

These questions are really asking how important money is to you. Can you reasonably expect your income from the career of your choice to satisfy your desires? Your career choice will have a bearing as to your probable life style. You may have to consider trade-offs between job satisfaction and probable financial rewards.

46.   Other career areas that interest me are:

From the preceding questions you should have received some insight into other areas of interest.

47. What do I really want from my career? (List in order of importance objectives such as job satisfaction, salary, working conditions, prestige, etc.)

By listing what you want from your career in order of your priorities, you are in a good position to evaluate careers suitable for you. Trade-offs are often necessary in making a career choice, but by arranging your individual priorities you will be better able to analyze how various careers fit your individual needs.

Perhaps the exercise of answering these questions simply reinforced your present career plans. This would be a strong indication that you have chosen an area in which you are likely to be happy and successful.

If you are having difficulty in making a career decision, I suggest you go over your answers with a friend. A friend who listens to your answers can be as helpful as most career consultants, and you will save approximately $50 per hour.

You should consider taking the completed questions to your school career counselor or one of the counselors at your state employment service. Listen to their evaluations of your needs. But also remember that your career choice should be yours. Others can help you in making a decision, but the final choice is yours alone.

Now that you have areas of interest, you should start considering specifics. Your school career guidance center or school library will have books that can help you in making a choice.

The U.S. Department of Labor publishes a *Dictionary of Occupational Titles,* which lists many thousands of jobs available in areas you may never have known existed. You will also learn of jobs that suit your present level of skill. The U.S. Department of Labor also publishes an *Occupational Outlook Handbook,* which predicts future employment needs. Doubleday and Company publishes an *Encyclopedia of Careers and Vocational Guidance,* which covers employment outlook, earnings, work conditions, special requirements, methods of entering, advancement, and special educational requirements. J.G. Ferguson Publishing Company publishes a *Concise Handbook of Occupations,* which includes 305 of the more popular jobs, with requirements from an eighth grade education to a doctoral degree. Robert R. Knopp publishes a *Guide to Careers Through Vocational Training* by Edwin Whitfield and Richard Hoover. This book gives meaningful data on jobs, including those requiring little or no formal training. It gives wage range, starting salary, and fringe benefits as well as what the job entails, preparation, and training plus the physical and personal traits required.

From these books you will find that functions you perform in one job may be well suited for jobs you might have previously considered completely unrelated. Thus you will see that alternatives are available. A career choice doesn't have to be cast in concrete. The education and training requirements of most jobs are also applicable to other career areas. If your interests change or you find you have made a poor choice, a change in career direction does not necessarily mean starting all over again from scratch.

You should keep in mind that just getting career training is not enough. To start on a career, a job is necessary. Besides the job market information available from the listed sources, your guidance counselor can provide you with current information. Because the job markets do change, you should consider alternative career possibilities.

For further help in making career decisions, you should contact people in the career area that interests you. Ask them about their work. Generally people are flattered to be approached by someone who needs help in making a career decision. You might find that a career you considered glamorous loses some glitter, while other careers gain in excitement.

You could also approach a firm in your career area and tell them of your interest. Ask for a part-time or summer job. If you are successful, this will give you a good gauge to judge your future career choice. (See Chapter 10, p. 115 for a discussion of how to obtain an interview for a part-time or summer job.)

You can write to professional and trade associations. They can be of great help in supplying you with detailed information about work in their career areas as well as the anticipated employment outlook.

You must be careful that your choice is not dictated by the fact that a particular career requires little special training or is easy. An easy job can become very boring. If your career is not personally challenging, you could easily become a clock watcher whose high point of the day is the time he can go home.

The same holds true for money. Don't make a career choice solely because of financial reward. Money, after a while, becomes less important unless the job continues to remain challenging to you. Many college graduates take their first full-time job in areas other than that which they had planned as their career choice. The main reason given by these graduates for taking this first job was "more money." However, surveys made of people who voluntarily leave their first job show that money was listed as the main reason by fewer than 10 per cent. Reasons such as not being able to utilize training and boredom were cited far more often. You can see from these facts that while the recent graduate is influenced greatly by financial reward as to the first job, financial reward loses importance when measured against job satisfaction.

Chances are that economics will demand that you spend a great deal of your life working. If you don't like your work, you are going to be unhappy. When you hate the thought of getting out of bed and going to work, your career has become your prison. If this is the case, you can look forward to possible ulcers, hypertension, and even an early heart attack. Career happiness does affect your overall health. On the other hand, if you look forward to your work and enjoy it, you are going to be happy and are more likely to be healthy.

You are not going to find a career in which every aspect brings great joy, but I like to evaluate jobs in terms of a "happiness" quotient. I have had a large number of graduates rate their job happiness on a scale of 1 to 10, with 10 being the highest, and also supply me with income and other information. I discovered that there is no apparent correlation between income and happiness in terms of enjoying one's career. The trite phrase, "money isn't everything," seems to hold true for job satisfaction.

I did find some interesting correlations in that unhappy people tend to be considering a career change, hold their employers in lower esteem, and showed considerably less loyalty to their employers. Among those graduates showing a high happiness quotient, I found that the majority of them felt that their job fulfilled basic needs of recognition and self-esteem.

Some students, in particular older ones, frequently feel that their career decisions have already been made and are not going to change. It must be realized that this is an age of swiftly changing technology. While career fields unheard of just a few years ago are opening up, many other careers are becoming obsolete. Retraining for career change has become necessary for many thousands of people. Now is really the time to consider the possible alternatives that are available which can utilize skills and training presently being developed or acquired. Often, with only slight modification of your planned curriculum, you can open the doors to several alternative career areas.

A pitfall to avoid in making career decisions is to categorize careers by sex. Don't discard careers that meet your needs by placing labels on them such as "a man's job" or "a woman's job." We are seeing these psychological barriers break down rapidly. You should adopt a career choice based on your own needs today and not on former sexist ideas of what are "proper jobs."

The same open mind holds true for minorities. The major reason for exclusion from career fields today is not prejudice. It is the fact that minority members frequently consider areas closed to them because of attitudes that existed in the past. Because of these ideas, many are not obtaining the training necessary for entry into these areas.

While you should start planning the direction you want your education to take as soon as possible, you should realize that it is very possible your interests will change. Classes you take, instructors, friends, special interests, and experiences might cause you to modify and even completely change your original educational and career objectives. Your original career choice should not be inflexible. You should be open to change, but only when the change will better meet your own individual needs. You should not let anyone else dictate a career change.

In making your career and educational plans, you should consider all of the aspects covered, but most of all you should "consider."

Chapter 2
Goal Setting

Today we hear a great deal about management by objective. This is nothing really new; it is simply goal setting—setting realistic goals for the future and measuring how they have been met.

Without goals your life would have no real meaning. Chances are you have known hard-working people who, shortly after retirement, seemed to wither and die in a very short time. These were people who worked a lifetime striving for goals. When they retired, they felt they were through. They stopped reaching for greater improvement. They failed to maintain goals, and without goals there is no purpose to life and it does not last.

Goals are a blueprint, a map, a plan for your future. You wouldn't consider driving from Miami to Seattle without a road map. The same should hold true for your life.

Without goals you are not going to really get started in any direction. Imagine yourself in a race without a finish line. You are not going to be motivated to keep on running without that line up ahead telling you how far you have to go to succeed. Meaningful goals are motivators that keep us striving for ever-greater achievements.

Just setting goals is not enough. They must be goals you want to meet. The only real motivation for continued effort is self-motivation. Your goals must be what you want to reach, not what someone else wants you to reach. Many people tend to adopt ideas of other people as their own. Since these are not really their own ideas, such people are not strongly motivated to succeed. You must learn to "follow your own drummer."

By now you should either have specific career goals in mind or have one or more general ideas as to your future career. Possibly you have several alternative career goals in mind. With your career goals in mind you can define the steps or interim goals that you will meet in order to obtain your career goal.

First, analyze your career goal functionally. What will you really be doing when you reach this goal? Now, answer these few simple questions.

Formal Educational Goals

1. What education (degrees and/or special courses) can I obtain that will be of help in attaining my career goal?

Working Skill Goals

2. What skill improvement is necessary for me to reach my career goal?

3. What additional skills can I learn that will help me to reach my career goal?

Experience Goal

4. What additional experience will help prepare me for my career goal? (Be specific.)

The goals that these questions reveal are really steps or plateaus to reach in your career ascent. You have decided where you want to be in 20 years, and now you are simply deciding the best way of getting there.

The steps you strive for should fall into a logical sequence. The same steps might, however, fit many possible career goals. A degree in mechanical engineering could be a step toward entering corporate management, becoming a patent attorney, going into engineering design work, or becoming a consultant, to name just a few positions.

In the same way that educational training can be used for different career goals, so can other types of training be utilized for the same career goal. A goal to be president of a large corporation might be met by people with diverse training such as law, marketing, engineering, or finance.

If you are undecided between alternative careers, whenever possible your interim goals should be applicable to both career choices. If your steps or interim goals are not related to your career goal, you may attain many short-term goals but fail to achieve your career goal. Therefore it is necessary to lay out your steps. What goals should be attained to meet your career goal, and in what order should they be reached?

Assume that your desire is to have your own retail clothing business. Your goals might be as shown in the diagram.

12 yr.	I will have opened my own clothing store.
10 yr.	I will have two years' experience in managing a clothing store, including buying experience.
8 yr.	I will have three years' experience in retail management positions, which will have included work in personnel functions, advertising, sales management, bookkeeping, and stock control.
5 yr.	I will obtain a retail trainee position with a retail clothing chain or department store and will learn basic operational procedures.
4 yr.	I will obtain a bachelor's degree in business administration with emphasis on marketing.
4 yr.	I will progress to retail sales and will have two years' experience in clothing sales.
2 yr.	I will obtain part-time and summer positions in a retail clothing store and will learn stock work.

If opening your own clothing store was your career goal, the other goals were interim goals. Each of these interim goals could be further broken down to many lesser goals. As an example, while working part-time in clothing sales and going to school you could have such goals as:

> I will increase my weekly sales from a current average of $800 to $1000 by the end of the semester. I will accomplish this by suggestive selling and by paying attention to the customers' reactions.

> Without assistance, I will be able to measure and mark a suit for alterations by the end of the semester. I will accomplish this by working with the tailor and the manager during slow periods.

> I will work on the next inventory and understand the procedure so that I will be able to conduct a future inventory without assistance.

The goals or objectives you set for yourself should be included in one of the following four categories:

> New Learning Goals—A learning experience or accomplishment that is new to you.
> Improvement Goals—An improvement in some project you are now doing, such as work habits or skills.
> Problem Solving Goals—Obtaining a solution for a problem.
> Personal Goals—Improving an area of human relations.

Goals don't have to be specifically related to a job. You might have goals for the school term such as:

a. I will complete the sociology paper on African mores and turn it in at least one week prior to the May 1 deadline (new learning goal).
b. I will join at least one club or organization by the end of the term (personal goal).
c. I will attend at least five campus cultural events this term (concerts, art exhibits, and special lectures) (new learning goal).
d. I will learn the names of at least eight fellow students in each of my classes (personal goal).

e. I will raise my grades in German from the current C to a B by the end of the term. I will accomplish this by joining the German Club on campus and thus spend time with German-speaking students (problem solving goal and improvement goal).

f. I will complete an entry for the science exhibit (new learning goal).

g. I will obtain no less than a 3.6 grade point average this term (improvement goal).

h. I will have fewer than three grammatical errors on my English term paper (improvement goal).

Your goals should always be stated in specific, measurable terms. It must be absolutely clear whether a goal has or has not been met.

Your goals should always be put down in writing. By writing your goals you are consciously defining them. Writing the goals reinforces the need for them and triggers self-motivation. Also, when you have formally written goals, it makes it more difficult to make excuses about why your goals were not met.

Goals should be periodically re-evaluated, since the relevancy of a goal may change. You should not make a goal a "commandment" but should be flexible as you and your needs change. You should set realistic time tables for accomplishing your goals, and the time tables should also be reviewed and re-evaluated.

A key to success in meeting goals is the management of time. All of us have the same amount of time to utilize, but our accomplishments within the time vary greatly. Ben Franklin learned how to account for his time through a series of daily goals. Each night he would prepare these daily goals for the next day. These were things he wanted to do. He then reviewed his accomplishments for that day and compared them with the goals he had set the night before. If he did not meet a goal he asked himself why it wasn't met. Some of his goals were only to devote a period of time to some endeavor. By writing his goals out he was forced to evaluate his daily accomplishments critically. He didn't like being critical about his daily accomplishments, as he had quite an ego. But by using the daily goals as a motivator, he maximized the use of his time. He was able to be successful in many areas, such as printer, inventor, writer, publisher, and statesman.

You may not be another Ben Franklin, but if you set daily goals and follow them, you will find you are able to get a great deal more accomplished in one day than you felt possible. By setting daily goals you will reach your intermediate goals, and if your intermediate goals are relevant to your career goal, then that too is within your reach. The Chinese have a proverb: "A journey of a thousand miles starts with the first step." Accomplishing your career goal should start now.

Goals may be redefined, and routes to reach them may change, but without goals, you will drift aimlessly. Don't leave to chance that which is within your grasp.

Chapter 3

Preparing For Success

Success requires motivation. It is not enough to wish for something; you must be motivated to work for it.

If your goals are meaningful to you, they will serve as motivators for your efforts. If, however, your goals mean little to you, it is going to be hard to get enthusiastic about your college work. If this is the case, a re-evaluation of goals is in order.

If you associate with people who are motivated to achieve their goals, you will find that they reinforce your own motivation. We tend to see ourselves the same way we see our dominant peer group. We often pattern ourselves after our friends. If your friends are negative people with a "what's the use, the whole world is going to hell" attitude, you can expect this negativism to affect you. You can see the importance of choosing friends and groups that can be of help.

A positive attitude is necessary for motivation and success. If you have doubt about your ability, your level of effort reflects this doubt. Unfortunately, most of us tend to be more negatively motivated than we are positively motivated. Dr. Maxwell Maltz points this out in his excellent book *Psycho-Cybernetics.*

How many times have you heard students say, "I'm lousy in math." By repeating it often enough, they firmly believe it. No matter how much instruction they receive, they are going to reject it. They have become negatively reinforced. By saying they can't do something and then failing when they try, they have created a self-fulfilling prophesy.

It is not necessary to be negatively motivated. When my son first tried water skis he fell flat on his face. When he got back to the dock he said, "See me, I almost got up on my feet!" He was positively motivated by an attempt that most people would have viewed as a disaster. He wanted to succeed and saw some success in his first attempt. By continuing to believe he could succeed, he kept trying until he was successful.

Role playing can be used to put yourself in a positive frame of mind. Actors sometimes find that when they are playing a role it affects their personal life. They have become the character they are playing. In these cases role playing was unconscious. It is possible to consciously change to the person you would like to become by role playing.

As an aid to role playing list the characteristics you would like to have:

1._____
2._____
3._____
4._____
5._____
6._____
7._____
8._____

For each of these characteristics list at least two situations in which you feel you have exercised these characteristics:

1.   a._____
      b._____

2.   a._____
      b._____

3.   a._____
      b._____

4.   a._____
      b._____

5.   a._____
      b._____

6.   a._____
      b._____

7. a._____
    b._____

8. a._____
    b._____

Now you can see that the role you wish to play isn't really so different from who you are now. You should consciously try to do things the way this person you wish to be would do them. In your daily life ask yourself how the character you are playing would handle the situation. After a while you will find you are no longer acting. You have become the character you were playing.

In the song "Whistle a Happy Tune" from the musical *The King and I*, Anna sings, "When I fool the people I fear, I fool myself as well." What Anna is saying, of course, is that by role playing she herself can believe the part she is playing.

People who cannot dance well can frequently dance very well under hypnosis. Their minds under hypnosis have been purged of past failures. So if you can think of yourself as a success, if your self-image is positive, you can be successful.

A new face can change a person's self image. There have been many cases of people who were unhappy with their appearance. They regarded themselves in low esteem before plastic surgery. After surgery their self-image changed. They liked themselves. With the change in their self-esteem they found whole new avenues open to them that previously they believed to be closed. Plastic surgery didn't really do anything other than change their packaging a little. The real change is what they did for themselves. Their personal outlook as to their own worth changed, and when they acted as if they respected themselves, other people showed respect toward them.

If you want other people to like you, you must first learn to like yourself. The only way you are going to like yourself is through self-esteem. For a good self-image it helps to reinforce your successes. Talk over successes, no matter how small, with a friend, your spouse, or parents. You want a person who will be positive. This positive reinforcement will not only help your self-image but also will reinforce your desire for future successes. You will find that the more you achieve, the better your self-image will be. You will find that as your grades improve, your desire for further improvement will increase. Nothing seems to help success like success.

As an aid to a good self-image you can list what you believe to be your strong personal assets and your reasons for considering them so:

_____

_____

Reasons:_____

_____

_____

_____

Reasons:_____

_____

_____

_____

Reasons:_____

_____

_____

_____

Reasons:_____

_____

It is not egotistical to like yourself. The fact that you have faults shouldn't stop you from liking yourself. We all have imperfections, but this doesn't mean we're not worthwhile human beings.

Liking yourself does not mean you should ignore your faults. Only by recognizing them and admitting that these are problem areas can you work to improve.

The simple act of listing what you consider to be your faults or problem areas and then listing ways of improving will serve as a motivator to improve and bring your faults into proper perspective.

Personal problem areas:

_____

_____

Ways to improve:_____

_____

_____

_____

_____
_____
Ways to improve:_____
_____
_____

_____
_____
Ways to improve:_____
_____
_____

_____
_____
Ways to improve:_____
_____
_____

_____
_____
Ways to improve:_____
_____
_____

If you were not a person of ability you would not have gone as far as you have. The attitude that you can succeed and, more important, that you will succeed mean far more than heredity, environment, or even I.Q. You are capable of succeeding in both college and life.

NOTES

Chapter 4

Planning Your Curriculum

Your parents might have thought you would never make it, but here you are in college. You don't have it made yet because you have quite a way to go.

You might feel as if you are in a gigantic maze. There are many different ways to go, and you are not sure which way is best for you. Before you start planning your courses for the next few years, which will get you through your maze, you should understand the following terms:

Electives. Non-required courses for a major or degree. They are used to fill in the total number of credits required for graduation.

General Education Courses (or Breath Courses). Required lower division courses. These courses are required for all students in order to graduate. They fulfill your needs as an educated person in helping you to understand and appreciate the arts and sciences as well as provide training in the ability to analyze, make decisions, and communicate. These courses are people-oriented rather than directly related to a vocation. They help to make you a well-rounded person.

Lower Division Courses. These are general education courses of a preparatory and survey nature, normally taken during the first two years of college.

Upper Division Courses. These are in-depth courses normally taken during the junior and senior years.

Major. Primary field of study or specialization. A major consists of a specified number of upper division subjects in a particular area of study. Units used for a major generally cannot also be used to meet general education requirements.

Minor. A secondary field of study. It consists of a lesser number of credits in a field of study.

Associate Degree (AA). A two-year degree normally obtained from a two-year college. It requires approximately 60 semester units or 90 quarter units. (Includes general education requirements.)

Bachelor's Degree (BA). Usually the traditional four-year degree, requiring approximately 120 semester units or 180 quarter units.

Quarter Unit x 2/3 = Semester Unit

Semester Unit x 1½ = Quarter Unit

Master's Degree (MA). Varies from about 16 to 36 semester units or 24 to 54 quarter units (based on school and area of study). It takes approximately one to two years beyond a bachelor's degree. A thesis or special project is also normally required.

Doctoral Degree (PhD). Normally takes about three years beyond the bachelor's degree. Generally requires courses plus a thesis.

Your advisor probably recommended that you take 14 to 18 units per semester. Generally this is considered a full load. Special permission is usually required to carry more than 21 units in one semester.

While five or six courses may seem like a lot, studies have shown that the average student who carries more units than normal does not suffer in grades. Therefore the average course load is not too much even for your first term.

With approximately 120 semester units to be earned for your bachelor's degree (or approximately 60 for your AA degree) you must carry an average of approximately 15 units per semester. By checking your school catalog you will see your exact credit requirements.

You should also check your school catalog for general educational requirements. Assume your school requires 40 units of general education courses. Since these are considered lower division courses and are therefore taken during the first two years, you will have approximately 20 semester units of electives for these two years.

If you are either in a two-year college or intend to transfer to another four-year college you should obtain a catalog from the school to which you want to transfer. You want to make sure that you fulfill that school's general educational requirements. You should also check with the registrar of the school to which you intend to transfer. You can thus find out in advance what courses will or won't be accepted from your school. Some schools require that certain of their general education courses be taken at their school.

Just because a course has the same or a similar title does not mean it is the same course as offered by another school. This is particularly important in dealing with courses that are prerequisites for other courses. These courses are building blocks that make up the foundation for more advanced study. If a school does not consider a course equivalent to one of their prerequisites, they are unlikely to accept it. Your guidance office can supply you with information about what many particular schools will or will not accept. There is no uniformity among colleges regarding course titles and course content. In many cases the difference exists even within colleges in the same state system. By checking the prerequisites for your planned upper division courses, you will be able to get many of these courses out of the way during your first two years.

Within your required general educational courses you still have a great deal of leeway. That is, you often have choices from large groups of courses. As an example, a physical science course may be required. Your choices might be astronomy, chemistry, geology, and meteorology. You should first of all consider which if any are prerequisites for your planned major. If none is required for your major, you should then consider which will help you the most. Let us assume that you want to go into radio or television news. Meteorology, in this instance, would probably be the best course for you, as it would be extremely valuable in weather forecasts.

Assume you require three courses in the social science fields. Your choices might be in anthropology, economics, geography, history, political science, philosophy, psychology, or sociology. If you were going to be a business major, economics as well as psychology would probably interest you. If you were planning on becoming a minister, perhaps philosophy, psychology, or sociology would interest you.

Assume you just don't really know what you want to major in. You may be an undeclared major taking a general course or have declared a major but feel that it may not really be what you want. You should consider taking general education courses that interest you the most as well as electives that interest you. Nearly every department has general overview or survey courses. You should take these courses as a sampling device. By taking these courses early in your college career, you will be able to make a decision about your course of study. Some students feel that since they have not made up their minds, they should take a breather. They take off a year, intending to come back. Because of marriage, jobs, or other obligations, most never return. If you decide to take off a year, you should realize that the odds are that you won't return to college.

Let us assume you want very much to go to law school, but you don't know at this time whether or not family finances will permit you to go. Assume you majored in American history, political science, or English. (There is no real pre-law requirement other than a four year degree.) If you do not enter law school, you will have a degree that generally will not stand by itself. That is, you will have a degree that by itself will not prepare you for a career or make you otherwise a highly desirable commodity on the employment market. On the other hand, if you had a bachelor's degree in a field such as engineering, accounting, communications, geology, or chemistry, you would really have an interim career goal. You wouldn't be just another of the generally educated unemployed. If you did graduate from law school, you would have a very valuable specialized combination. As examples: geology and law would prepare you for specialized work in mining law, engineering and law prepares you for patent law, and accounting and law prepares you for tax law.

If your first degree can stand by itself, you have a worthwhile product even if you are unable to go to graduate school. In other words, this type of degree is like an insurance policy, protecting you against unforeseen events that might prevent you from continuing your education. If you feel that such events are likely, you should consider the economic relevance of your first degree. Naturally if finances will not be a problem in your life, personal enrichment courses and majors should certainly be considered.

The same holds true for community college AA degrees. If you feel that you might not be able to go on to a four-year degree, a great deal of thought should be given to a two-year degree that will be economically meaningful.

Many students never even consider vocational programs. Certainly at one time blue collar workers were not college graduates and normally made less money than white collar workers, and no matter how highly skilled they were, nevertheless were treated as being "lower class." Major changes have taken place in recent years. Many vocationally trained people earn more than the average college graduate. These skilled technicians today are a needed part of our community. Don't turn down the thought of one of the many vocational fields open to you just because it doesn't fit your conception of an "educated person." This is especially important if you feel that you will not be able to complete a traditional four-year college degree.

In planning your classes, don't try to bunch up all your classes one right after the other in three days in order to have two days off. Leave some breathing space. Allow for some time to relax, study, organize, and eat. Some students take classes they are not particularly interested in because these courses fit into this type of compact schedule. What the class will do for you is far more important than a tight little schedule.

After you have made some friends on campus, you will get a lot of advice such as, "take a course from Smith because he gives no assignments and everyone gets at least a B." Or, "don't take classes from Jones unless you don't mind working your head off for a C." Everyone is going to have opinions about instructors, and you will find that different people view the same instructor differently. Most instructors have some students who feel they are the greatest and some students who feel they are the worst. Don't accept other people's opinions. Since you are going to college to learn to think for yourself, try to be your own person now.

In the same vein, don't take classes just because they are easy. An easy course or teacher that does little to improve you is not worthwhile. Time and money are being invested in your education, so you should be interested in getting the most from this investment.

If you plan on graduate school, you should know what average will be required of you for admittance. This will give you a goal to aim for, which is an incentive for better work. Should it become clear that you will be unable to enter a graduate school, you can plan early for alternative courses of study.

Besides the average for graduate school admittance, you should know what average you must keep to stay in school as an undergraduate as well as the average needed to graduate (usually a 2.0 point).

Some courses are graded on a pass-fail basis. These courses are not computed into your grade point average. So, if it is necessary to raise your grade point average, such a course will not help you.

Assume that you want to go to medical school. If you find for any reason that you will not be able to be admitted, you have not necessarily wasted four years unless you let them be wasted. There are a number of areas open to you utilizing much of your training, such as chemistry, pharmacy, dentistry, podiatry, veterinary medicine, optometry, biology, etc.

You should realize that alternative careers are available. If you are unable or uninterested in continuing a course of study, you should consider the alternatives available. Many courses required for one major are also required for other majors. While a change in your major should not be made lightly, you can usually make the change and utilize much of what you have already taken either for required courses or for electives.

Just as your undergraduate degree can make a graduate degree more valuable, so can a minor reinforce a major and make it more valuable. An English major by itself doesn't seem like an economically desirable degree, but if it were coupled with a minor in journalism, advertising, or communications, it would take on a completely new meaning. A minor in computer sciences would make an accounting major more desirable. A major in psychology and a minor in music could prepare you for a career in music therapy. The combination of a major and a minor can add a completely new dimension to your education. By taking different electives, obtaining different minors and exercising different choices for general educational and major subjects, it is possible for two students to obtain the same degree yet have a completely different academic emphasis.

In planning your minors you should consider what the minor will do for your major. If you are interested in a minor that is completely unrelated to your major, perhaps you should be giving thought to a new minor, or possibly even a different major.

While some majors require minors, others do not. If you are unable to obtain a minor, you can still use your electives to give additional strength to your major or to an allied field.

If you are having difficulty in the introductory course in your major, it could be because of poor preparation in high school. Perhaps you should reconsider your major. Poor grades could be caused by lack of interest, which certainly indicates that you made a poor choice or lack a natural ability required for the course. Of course, you may just require a remedial course in the area that is giving you difficulty.

It has been estimated that over 40 per cent of all graduates end up in career fields other than their first declared major. Your interests are likely to change. The courses you take have a sifting and winnowing effect. By discarding the chaff, you will be able to find the field that is right for you.

Parents frequently force students into the wrong major. In trying to help, they push their ideas about what is best. Unfortunately, they frequently misconstrue the needs of the individual student. Even when they are right, some students rebel and change their course of study, not so much because of their own interests, but because, by not accepting a parent's choice, they feel they are either retaliating and getting even or showing their independence. You should not automatically reject suggestions because they were offered by your parents.

If there is a family business, employment problems may be eliminated. You should think of how your interests fit into the business. Assume your family owns a machine shop. Some of the majors that would fit in with the business would be in marketing, employee relations, general business management, accounting, or engineering.

Many schools today allow you to construct your own major. Your career goal might not fit in with the established majors. If this is the case, you should check with your guidance counselors.

In your career choice you should, of course, consider marketability of your training. Today there are many education majors working as sales clerks or taxi drivers. They wanted to teach, but because fewer children are being born and because there has been an increase in teaching programs, we have a huge surplus of education majors. However, even in overcrowded fields such as teaching, there are still specialized areas in which teachers are in demand. Therefore, you should consider marketability when choosing majors and minors.

It is possible to obtain two majors, or dual majors. This is especially feasible when many of the courses for one major are also required for another. Generally these majors are closely allied.

It is also possible to be enrolled at more than one college at the same time. This dual enrollment normally does not require any special permission, but you should be concerned about transferability of courses to the school from which you desire your degree. If a course closely duplicates a course you have already taken, you will not receive credit for it.

Today many students take five years rather than the traditional four years to obtain their bachelor's degree. Other students shorten their education by taking heavy unit loads and attending summer sessions. Your paramount concern should not be how long you will have to remain in school but what is going to be best for you.

It may not be necessary to actually take the number of credits or courses usually required for graduation. If you take the CLEP test (College Level Examination Program), you can receive up to two years' college credit for what you already know. These tests are given at many colleges and universities. Also, many schools give college credits just for having been in military service. In addition, courses you may have taken in service might allow you college credit. The *Guide to the Evaluation of Educational Experiences in the Armed Forces*, published by the American Council on Education, shows the recommended college credits for various government schools and correspondence courses. Many schools follow this guide.

In addition, if you feel that you know the subject matter of a course, it is often possible to challenge the course by examination. With permission you can take an examination to receive credit for a course without actually taking the course. Information about challenging a course is available from your college registrar.

Your curricula decisions must be made by you. No one else should make them for you, nor would you want this. If you make your decisions based on your own needs, they will be good for you.

Chapter 5

How to Study

Chances are you made it through high school without having to develop good study techniques. Your competition in high school included many students who had no intention of ever going to college, and many of your fellow students were not motivated. With this type of competition, a moderate amount of study probably allowed you to earn grades that were sufficient to get you into college. Now, however, you are going to have to prove yourself all over again against far greater academic competition.

Admission to most graduate schools today is limited. Your grade point average will affect your future. Even if grad school is not your goal, in a tight job market employers are able to pick and choose. The better job offers generally go to the top students as evidenced by their academic record.

MAKING A SCHEDULE

To succeed you are going to have to learn how to get the most out of the time available for study. In short, you are going to have to set up a study schedule and learn how to study.

Your first step should be to decide how to allocate your study time. To do this, make a chart covering a full week, as shown in the accompanying diagram. You should now fill in this chart with your class time. If you are working, your work hours should also be shown. The areas that are blank can be devoted to either study or other activities.

You should designate specific days and times for study of specific subjects. Plan on studying at least two hours for each hour of class time. Therefore, if you are taking 15 hours of classes, you should plan on studying 30 hours, or a total of 45 hours per week devoted to education. You will find that some courses won't require two hours of study for every hour in

	Monday	Tuesday	Wednesday	Thursday	Friday	Saturday	Sunday
7 AM							
8:00							
9:00							
10:00							
11:00							
12 Noon							
1 PM							
2:00							
3:00							
4:00							
5:00							
6:00							
7:00							
8:00							
9:00							
10:00							

class, but other subjects may require a great deal more time. As each school term progresses you will find that adjustments will be necessary. Your allocation of time for each course might be changed, but be very careful about reducing the total time allocated for study. Study at specific times should become a habit.

Study should be your number one priority, and if it is necessary to change your schedule and cut out some study time, you must be sure you are able to gain that study time back by taking from some other activity.

Your schedule should make every hour important. It should show recreation and relaxation activities as well as time for meals and adequate sleep. In order to unwind, you should plan for recreation just as you plan for study. It is a necessary part of your total plan. By sticking to your study plan, you will enjoy your relaxation and recreation time much more because you will not feel guilty. You will know that you have earned the time off.

In your schedule, you should consider utilizing periods between classes and short breaks. You must realize that all of your time is valuable.

If you are employed, your study schedule will have to be adjusted around your work schedule as well as your class schedule. Because this reduces the net time available for study you may find you have to schedule every available minute. Your lunch and coffee breaks at work can be used for study. Studying during these short periods can quickly become a natural habit.

If you commute to and from work or school in public or private transportation, these periods can likewise be utilized. When you are driving you can use the time to try to recall and reconstruct the last lecture (always, of course, giving the major part of your concentration to the road). This exercise in recall will reinforce your learning.

Married students should not neglect their families. While education is important, it should not be at the expense of normal family life. Time should actually be scheduled for family activities. If you feel your school is seriously affecting your family life, you should consider a reduced academic schedule.

In planning your schedule you should think of studying while you are alert. Don't plan on using late hours when you have to force yourself to stay awake.

As you will see, retention of material will be much better if you spread out your studying time. Therefore your schedule should generally provide for study periods of no more than an hour at a time for a given subject, and preferably 30 to 45 minutes.

Whenever possible you should avoid studying closely related subjects in sequence, as this can lead to confusion.

If you schedule your "toughest" assignment first, you will get a feeling of accomplishment when you are done, and the rest of your study will seem much easier.

Term projects such as term papers and additional books to be read should be worked into your study plan as soon as they are assigned. In this way you won't have to devote a great deal of time to these projects at the end of the term, when you should be involved in review.

Planning your work prevents things from piling up, and if work piles up you will find yourself in a situation where you will be under pressure. Generally, studying under pressure is not as effective as studying on a normal study plan. When you are not under pressure, the work becomes more interesting; and when there is interest, retention will be increased.

A study plan should be detailed. It should cover not only what subject is to be studied but also the area of the subject and how it is to be studied. Therefore, in addition to the general weekly plan for the term you should have a refined plan for specific days. If a plan is not detailed, it would be possible to put more time in areas of great interest and avoid other areas completely.

A detailed plan for one day's study might look like the one shown in the box. By adhering to your schedule you will find yourself unable to avoid unpleasant tasks. Procrastination will become exceedingly difficult.

Tuesday, February 27

9:00-9:30 AM Art 10—Review accomplishments of Da Vinci and Chapters 7 and 8 of text.

1:00-2:00 PM English 1A—Scan and read Chapter 6 of text (½ hour). Check periodical index for article on Presidential speech writing for term paper (½ hour).

2:00-3:00 PM Business Law 20A—Review Chapters A, B, C, 1, 2, and 3 for quiz. Review text (40 minutes). Reveiw class notes (20 minutes).

3:00-4:15 PM Political Science 1A—Scan and read assigned magazine articles on China (½ hour). Complete general outline for term paper: "What Will Be the Political Influence of the New Africa" (45 minutes).

4:15-5:00 PM Business Math—Review exercises in text for Lessons 11 and 12 (15 minutes). Complete exercises for Chapter 13 (30 minutes).

5:00-6:00 PM Dinner

6:00-7:00 PM Business Law—Review material for quiz with Sally and Ed.

7:00-10:00 PM R & R (rest and relaxation)

Your schedule should not be so inflexible that it cannot be changed. In fact, periodically you should re-evaluate your weekly study plan. You should ask yourself whether you are giving enough time to subjects. Is your study time effective? What can be done to improve your study techniques? While a study plan must allow some flexibility, you must remember that if you allow it to be changed too readily, it will soon be forgotten.

If you fail to set up a study plan, you can expect to fall behind on your assignments. If you fall behind, the only solution will be to cram. Even if you are successful, information learned quickly is also forgotten quickly. This can lead to major problems if the information being learned will be the basis for further study.

You must forget about your personal problems. If you can't get them out of your mind, you are going to be unable to get anything worthwhile out of your studying. A minute or two spent thinking of something very pleasant will help greatly in reducing anxiety prior to studying. Some students find that a few minutes of physical exercise prior to studying helps them to put their personal problems on the "back burner" so that effective study is possible.

PHYSICAL SETTING

A place to study is very important. One place is not just as good as another. You should have a comfortable, well-lighted area for study, with as few distractions as possible.

Your place of study should allow you to write easily, so that you can take notes as well as be able to spread out papers and books. (This generally precludes studying in a bed or easy chair.)

Avoid using a desk light with only one fluorescent bulb. The flicker can cause fatigue. Normally two-bulb fluorescents are adjusted to eliminate the flicker.

While fraternity and sorority houses as well as student housing offer many social advantages that are important in your development as a well-rounded person, they are generally very poor places to study. The more distractions a place offers, the more difficult it is to study. Your place for study should not be a place where friends can reach you readily, either in person or by phone. It should not be in proximity to a TV, since the Big Eye can easily lead you astray and off your study plan. Distractions and interruptions will lessen the effectiveness of the time you spend in study.

While studying outside certainly looks attractive on a nice day, the outside offers too many distractions. Everything from birds and bugs to wind, traffic, and people all will interfere with your concentration. In addition, the sun's glare can make studying exceedingly difficult.

You should avoid too warm a study spot, as high temperatures can make you very sleepy. The place should be comfortable but not so comfortable as to induce sleep. Eating a heavy meal before studying should be avoided, as it will help put you to sleep. Whenever you find yourself getting tired, a change of activity will frequently revive you. A short walk or a shower will also help to wake you up.

The tools you will generally need for study are a dictionary, textbook, colored pens, and a notebook. There will be times when scissors, cellophane tape, and a ruler will also be useful. If you can get in the habit of studying with a pen or pencil in your hand, you will be more likely to underline and take notes.

Have you ever noticed that when someone sits down at a table in a crowded library, about half the people at the table look up? People welcome an opportunity to be distracted. Those who do not look up are those who do not let outside events affect their train of thought. You must learn to ignore external stimulation.

One hour of study is not necessarily as valuable as another hour of study. If you were to study a subject for 10 hours straight you would get far more out of the first hour you spent than you would get from the last hour. After a while you would have trouble keeping your mind on the work. You would find yourself using up the time without really studying. It has been found that it is easier to concentrate for shorter periods of time. Therefore, your retention is much better when you spread out the learning process. Studying a subject 1/2 hour a day for seven days would give you much greater retention than if you spent 3½ hours studying at one stretch. It also seems to hold true that the faster you learn, the faster you forget. Thus you are going to be more effective if you study every day for shorter periods of time.

You can effectively break up your study time by taking a short rest every 30 to 45 minutes. Just having a drink of water, writing a short letter, or doing any small personal chore is all that is required. After the break, you should study a different subject. Changing subjects serves to revitalize your interest. The effectiveness of our study is also related to our interest in what we are studying. Chances are that in the past you were reading a text and suddenly realized you didn't know what you have been reading. Your mind had wandered off while you continued to read on line by line without any absorption. If you lose your place, you don't know what you have read and what you haven't.

When you read a novel, your mind seldom wanders. You are interested and pay attention. When you are finished, you can describe what you have read in great detail if you are asked. Often you can vividly remember what you have read for years afterward. It is possible to get the same results with a textbook as you get with a novel, but to do so you must be truly interested. If you understand the relevance of the material you are reading and can consider how the material relates to what you have previously learned, you can become interested and even enthusiastic. If this is the case, you will remember what you read with very little effort. The material must make enough of an impression on you to remember it. If you treat study as a hated task, the time you spend at it will not be very productive. You must think positively and strive to enjoy what you are doing.

Some schools have peer tutoring, in which more advanced students work with students who are having difficulty in their studies. The main benefit of the program is that it forces the student to pay attention to the material. Also, working with a fellow student is often more interesting than working alone, and thus more meaningful. Peer tutors are frequently available at no cost or at a very reasonable cost.

A good way to help reduce wasted study time is a "fine" system. After each period of study, you should estimate how much time you wasted with outside distractions or just daydreaming. You can then fine yourself the wasted time. In other words, pay yourself back the time you wasted by increasing your study time requirements. A reward system is also very effective whereby you can reward yourself with some desired activity when your planned work or project is accomplished.

TECHNIQUES

Now that you have time devoted to study as well as a place for study, you will need to learn proper study techniques.

I have laid out a simple four-step study plan to be used before the material is covered in class session. There is nothing unique about this system; these general ideas have been advocated for years. One of the most important points about the study system is that you should always study prior to your class in order to obtain the maximum benefit from the class.

Step 1: Scan. By a rapid skimming of the text material, reading the first sentence of each paragraph, it is possible to very quickly get the general gist of what the material is about. The first sentence of a paragraph usually contains the "meat" of the paragraph, while the rest of the paragraph gives the details.

Step 2: Read and Question. Prior to reading the chapter, read any questions at the end of the chapter. By doing so the answers will seem to "pop right up" as you read the text. As you read, after each paragraph you should ask yourself what the paragraph actually says and answer to yourself in our own words. When you finish each chapter, ask yourself what the chapter was really about and answer mentally.

Step 3: Recite. Read the material aloud if your study area permits. Again, ask yourself the same questions that you did in Step 2. This is one of the times that group study can be effective. The person reading can ask the others (who have each separately gone through Steps 1 and 2) the questions. If, for some reason, you are unable to read aloud, you should repeat Step 2 instead.

Step 4: Refresh. Immediately prior to your class period, you should devote 5 to 10 minutes on a quick brush-up of your assignment.

In your scanning process you should pay particular attention to the author's introduction and the index. These will help in giving you an advance understanding of what will be learned. If conclusions are included, these should be particularly noted, and in your reading you will be able to understand how the author builds up to the conclusions.

In using your text, you should underline what you consider important. A yellow accent pen also works well to emphasize. In the margins you can put "memory joggers"—key words that tell you what a paragraph is all about. You must be careful that you don't underline so much that your special emphasis becomes meaningless.

Captions under pictures and diagrams are frequently very important. Also, if the author has seen fit to use boldface type or italics, it means that he considered the material exceptionally important.

Vocabulary

Vocabulary is a problem area for many students. Reading will not improve vocabularly unless you take the time to look up the words. Do not look up words while you are reading, as it will completely break your concentration on the text. You can underline words not understood with a special color pen. After you have finished the chapter, look up the underlined words in the dictionary.

By writing each new word on a 3 × 5 card and carrying them with you and looking through them at odd moments, you will quickly master the words. When you have accomplished this, you should place the cards in a vocabulary file to be periodically reviewed (about once a month).

If you fully understand what prefixes mean (such as anti-, pro-, sub-) your task of improving your vocabulary will be much easier. Looking at words for their roots is also helpful in determining their meaning. As an example, knowing that the root *ped* is indicative of the word foot helps in understanding the meaning of words such as quadruped, orthopedic, pedometer, and pedestrian.

If your instructor has given other additional reading assignments, you should follow Steps 1 and 2 after you have completed your text reading assignment. Scan, then read. During Step 2, take notes on any ideas not covered in the text. In your notes, also include a short summary of the reading assignment in your own words. When you are finished, ask yourself why the assignment was given. Generally, review time will not permit you to go through the reading assignments again, so you are going to have to be able to rely on your notes.

READING ASSIGNMENTS

In courses such as English, you might have several novels or plays to read. I suggest that prior to reading the actual work you should read a synopsis of the book or play. There are many such summaries available at college bookstores. Even a classical comic book covering one of the classics will help provide a general understanding. When you understand what the book is about, your reading will be more interesting as well as far easier to understand. After each chapter it will help if, in your own words, you set forth the basic point of the chapter.

Most students feel that they read too slowly and envy speed readers. Unfortunately, the claims of some speed reading courses just are not true. You cannot read 2000 words a minute and still comprehend perfectly what you have read. As speed increases beyond a particular point for each person, his or her comprehension decreases.

If you form every word with your mouth, you certainly do need help in reading. A simple aid is to clamp a pencil firmly in your mouth while you read, until you can break the habit. Another bad habit to be overcome is moving the head from side to side as you read. Your head should remain stationary, and the eyes should do the moving.

Many people hear what they are reading as if they were talking to themselves. This is known as verbalizing. Even though one's lips are not moving, the verbalizing process does slow down reading ability. The visual process of reading need not be tied to an auditory process. Chances are your school has a remedial reading program. With help you will be able to read considerably faster than you can verbalize.

Speed in reading is going to vary greatly. Your familiarity with the material, the grammar used, your purpose for reading, and the difficulty of the ideas presented will all affect your reading rate. When you are reading to gather data, such as to write a paper, a scanning process is quite helpful. By reading the first sentence of each paragraph you can quickly cover irrelevant material and find that which is pertinent to your needs. If your book includes scientific data or formulas, your reading speed will be significantly reduced in order to comprehend what is being read.

If your text includes problems to be worked out, it is far more meaningful if you work them out yourself than if someone else gives you the answers or tells you how to do them. Your own involvement will help your memory.

Science

Studying science is a problem for many students. The basis of much of their trouble is the unusual vocabulary. Many familiar words are given different meanings within a scientific field. In addition, there are a great number of unfamiliar words that must be learned. Besides writing the new scientific words on your vocabulary cards, you should also include words with which you are familiar but which have different scientific meanings.

In studying science, you should watch for the scientific principles. Underline or use yellow accent pen for the principles in your text. In addition, make out 5 × 7 cards for each chapter, on which you set forth the scientific principles explained in the chapter. Study these principles in the same manner as you review your vocabulary cards. You should think about how each of the principles you have studied would be applied.

Scientific diagrams given in the text are generally important. After studying a diagram, close your eyes and try to visualize the diagram. If you have difficulty visualizing, attempt to reproduce the basic diagram on paper without referring to the text. When you are finished, check the text to see whether you are correct.

If you have difficulty with a particular scientific concept, you should go to the library, where you will find other texts that cover the same material. Frequently you will find that an explanation set forth in a different manner is all that is necessary to clarify a problem.

In studying science, you are integrating many separately learned facts. Because of this, much of what you learn can be classified as "building blocks." If you don't understand the foundation material, you cannot continue with further study, as it will only confuse you. Therefore, if you are having trouble, talk to fellow students or your instructor. The longer you delay in obtaining clarification, the farther behind you will become.

Prior to any laboratory session, you should read the lab manual so you will know what will be expected of you. In your science lab, you must learn to take your time and be meticulous. Check to see that your equipment is set up properly, and also, when possible, make a simple test to see that it is working properly. Follow your instructions precisely. Don't be "almost" exact. You should try to be as accurate as possible with the equipment available.

You should keep a notebook handy and record everything you do and the results. By going over your notes and recalling exactly what you did, you will be able to review your laboratory sessions.

A great aid in science courses is a thorough understanding of the metric system. If, during each day, you estimate temperatures in centigrade and various objects in grains, centimeters, and other metric units, you will soon learn to think in metric terms.

Math

Mathematics scares many students. Actually, math is simply learning a series of principles or formulas, and then plugging in given facts to the proper formula.

In studying mathematics, you must first read and fully understand the problem. Know what is being asked. You should then make a rough estimate of what the answer should be. In this way, if your answer differs significantly from the estimate, the chances are that either there is an error in calculations or you used a wrong formula.

You should get in the habit of doing your math assignments as if they were a test. This will help you greatly when you have an actual test. You should also make sure you fully understand why you are computing the answers in a particular manner. Making up a very simple problem of the same nature as a given problem will often reveal the correct mathematical formula.

Sometimes it is easier to find the proper equation if you put the problem into words and then substitute numbers. As an example, suppose the problem is:

Three houses sold together for $65,000. The second house sold for $1500 more than the first house, and the third house sold for $2000 more than the second house. What was the selling price of each house?

The equation in words would be:

House + (house + $1500) + (house + $3500) = $65,000

or

$$3X + \$5000 = \$65,000$$
$$3X = \$60,000$$
$$X = \$20,000$$
$$X + \$1500 = \$21,500$$
$$X + \$3500 = \$23,500$$

In working math problems, remember to prove your answer whenever possible. In the case above, by adding $20,000, $21,500 and $23,500, you would find they equal $65,000.

The most common math errors are simple ones, such as misplaced decimal points. Therefore, care should be taken. By being neat, writing numbers clearly, and having defined columns, you will significantly reduce your mathematical errors.

In studying math, it is necessary that you review previously learned material on a regular basis. If you are not constantly using an equation, you might quickly forget it. By budgeting approximately 45 minutes per week for reviewing previous material, you will have no trouble with a final examination.

Language, more than any other subject, should be studied aloud. This will help you with pronunciation. You should start by working with small groups of words at a time and try to familiarize yourself with the pronunciation and meaning. It is best to start with nouns. If you are able to apply the nouns you learn as labels for the various objects you use or see, it will give you an immediate sense of accomplishment.

Flash cards are available with words in English on one side and in the foreign language on the other. Going through these cards, looking at the foreign word and giving the English translation, as well as looking at the English word and giving the foreign translation, will help you master your vocabulary.

You should try to apply the new grammar rules as you learn them. You should also try to think in the new language. We tend to verbalize our thoughts in English. If you can start substituting words of the other language as you learn them, you will quickly master the vocabulary.

If your campus has language clubs where the language is spoken, you can get a great deal of benefit out of membership. In the same way it will help greatly if you try to converse with foreign students in your new language. Constant practice is very important. Your library probably has language records, which will supplement your class work.

If a local art theatre features foreign language films with English subtitles, these can help your pronunciation as well as sentence structure. As you get into the language, you should try to watch the movies without using the subtitles as a crutch.

MEMORIZATION

You are not going to memorize any textbook. Memorizing by rote is generally a time-consuming and time-wasting process. Modern education places less and less emphasis on sheer memorization. There are, however, times when a list of items will have to be memorized in perfect order. It may also be necessary to memorize definitions. Before any material is memorized, you should first fully understand the material. Memorization is a difficult task, and the longer the list to be memorized, the more difficult it becomes. There are several methods that can be used to make the process easier.

Some students apply a rhythm to a list to be memorized. They actually learn to sing the list as a tune. Chances are that you learned your ABC's in this manner, and, if asked to recite them now, you would still remember that rhythm you learned long ago.

Another method is to compose a sentence using the first letter or syllable of each word on the list to be memorized. Assume that taxes are due in two installments, the first due in November and delinquent in December and the second due in February and delinquent in April. By remembering "No Damn Fooling Around" you will know November, December, February and April.

A more sophisticated method of memorization itself requires the memorization of a master list of objects. As an example, you might memorize a list of animals. If you then had to remember a list of people's names in order, you would associate each person with the proper animal on your animal list. Suppose you were remembering a list of president's names. Assume No. 13 on your list of animals is rabbit and the president (No. 13) is Millard Fillmore. If you imagined President Fillmore riding on a rabbit, when you follow your list of animals and get to No. 13, you would immediately think of Fillmore, whom you would visualize on a rabbit.

Another technique that can help is to memorize lists alphabetically. Going through the alphabet and thinking of a letter will tend to spur your memory.

LECTURES   As stated, immediately prior to a lecture you should take a quick scan of the material to be covered by the lecture. Five minutes is normally sufficient, as you want simply to refresh your memory regarding what you have learned.

In your lecture class take a seat directly in front of the lecturer so that you are fairly close. In this way you will be able to see blackboard diagrams and slides as well as being able to understand clearly what is said.

It is very easy to day dream when you make yourself too comfortable, so you are more likely to pay attention to the instructor if you sit up straight.

By looking at the lecturer's face, your hearing will actually improve. By seeing the lecturer's lips, you are more apt to hear what *is* said rather than what you *expect* to be said.

If you are overly warm it is very easy to become sleepy. Remove heavy coats and sweaters. You should not eat a heavy meal prior to a lecture, as this will make it difficult for you to remain attentive.

You should not hesitate to ask your instructor questions if you find something confusing or requiring clarification. Don't worry about seeming stupid. Chances are that if something is confusing to you, it is also confusing to others. Don't, however, ask questions of a purely personal nature during class time, or questions that digress from the material being covered.

It is very easy to forget, so notes are a valuable tool with which to capture your instructor's thoughts. You should have a separate notebook for each class, preferably a looseleaf type, in which you can add or remove pages. You should take notes on one side of the paper only so that your notes can be spread out for review. Each lecture should be labeled with the date and the chapter of the text being covered. In this way you will be able to study text and lecture notes together for review.

You should try to write legibly. Nothing is worse than trying to review lecture notes and realizing that you don't understand what your notes mean. In addition, your notes should be in your own words, so that you will understand what they mean, rather than repeating the words of the lecturer. Don't worry about taking notes in sentences. A few words are adequate if they convey meaningful information.

Your notes should be clear enough so that by looking at them you will come up with the gist of the lecture. A simple outline format is good for note-taking. Don't try to take down everything the lecturer says. This is a common fault of most notes. By including too much, they become a cumbersome review tool. Since you have read the chapter in the text prior to the lecture, you would not repeat material covered by the text in the notes. Your notes should supplement the text, not replace it.

You should make notes of new material not covered in the text, as well as material given a different emphasis and personal opinions of the lecturer. When the lecturer writes on the blackboard, it means that he or she considers the material important. This material should be set forth in your notes. Often the lecturer will tell you what is important by using phrases such as: "Be sure to note that . . .", "the main point is . . .", or "the real reason for . . .". You can underline or use arrows——▶ or boxes⸺⸺⸺if you want special emphasis in your notes.

Because a lecturer talks at a rate much slower than the rate at which we comprehend, our minds tend to wander in other directions. The instructor might actually be saying something contrary to what we think without our noticing it. This is especially likely to happen if you have a slow or uninspiring instructor.

It is difficult to listen. How often have you been introduced to a person and two minutes later you have no idea what the person's name is? You were thinking of something else or not interested enough to really listen. The same holds true for lectures. You spend over one quarter of your life in school. That time will be wasted if you refuse to listen.

By asking yourself questions as the lecturer proceeds, you can keep your attention focused on the lecturer. Ask yourself, "Why did he say that?" "How does that apply to me?" "Where is the emphasis?" However, if you take too much time reflecting on what the lecturer has said, you very well might miss an important point.

Immediately after class, or as soon thereafter as possible, go over your lecture notes. If they are not clear, clarify them. Make sure that everything you feel is important is set forth in your notes.

Generally, it is not a good idea to rewrite or type your notes, since the additional benefit usually isn't worth the time spent. However, especially in science classes, this may be necessary to make your notes meaningful. It may also be necessary if your instructor is not organized and rambles. Most lecturers, however, follow a definite outline. Some students tape their instructor's lectures in lieu of taking notes. This is not a good idea, as tapes cannot be used readily for review. You can't review a tape. You must listen to the whole tape, which is an extremely time-consuming job. For a three-credit class, you might have over 50 hours of tapes.

Tapes can be used if you want to reinforce a lecture by repeating the tape at a time normally not considered for studying. Tapes could be played while you are driving or performing manual work. Do not take your regular study time to listen to the tapes, though, because your time can be more valuably used.

You should avoid absences, since when a class is missed, you have missed an opportunity to take notes. If someone has a tape of the lecture for you to review, that is great. Otherwise, meet as soon as possible after the lecture with, preferably, two good students. Go over the lecture with them from their notes. Just copying their notes is not enough. You must understand the instructor's emphasis and reasons for it. If the instructor is teaching several sections of a class, you may be able to make up the missed class by attending one of the other sections.

If you feel that you are not getting enough from an instructor, find out whether any other instructor is teaching the same class. Perhaps auditing another instructor's lectures will help you. You might check to see whether you can change classes. Keep in mind that a popular instructor who is entertaining isn't a good instructor unless the students are able to grasp an understanding of the material.

Once a week, on a regular basis, you should review all of your lecture notes from the beginning of the course up to that date. While time certainly dulls your memory, repetition helps it. The material which is oldest, therefore, is repeated the most in review.

REVIEW

Study is different from review. In our studies we learn new material, but in our review we are reinforcing and organizing material we have learned.

Many students who have not done their work all semester try to cram by studying blocks of previously unlearned material in a short period of time. Generally the results are not satisfactory, for the faster they try to learn, the faster they forget.

Group study generally is not very beneficial for initial learning. Group work can, however, be exceedingly valuable for review. To be worthwhile, all of the students must have studied independently. Not much can be expected of a group that is meeting together in ignorance. Four people is usually the maximum that should review together. Larger groups tend to become too cumbersome. One person should take charge of the review. Otherwise organized progression is difficult. As an example, the group could go through the lectures with one person telling what he or she considers to be the main points or ideas. Other students could supplement this with their understanding of the lectures. Another valuable exercise for the group would be to try to determine what questions the instructor could ask for each chapter. This is really role playing based on your experiences with the instructor.

A strong advantage of group review is that you are more likely to remain attentive when you are working with your peers, and you will thus be able to devote far more time to the subject without your mind wandering off as is common in individual review sessions. The group forces your attention in much the same way a tutor would.

A disadvantage of a group review is that if the leader

does not exercise control, it can degenerate into a "bull session" with limited benefits.

While you are reviewing your lecture notes, you should also review the text material in order to tie the ideas or material together. A quick scan of your text should be easy, now that you have underlined important areas and added notes in the margin. If it is a laboratory course, you should, of course, review your lab notes.

By learning and practicing properly planned study and review, you will increase your chance for better grades as well as reduce the academic pressure of college.

After obtaining good grades on a few tests, some students tend to feel they have it made. College isn't so hard. They find that they had studied a great deal of material that wasn't even on the examinations. They "get smart" and feel they can reduce their level of effort. They may even try to psych out the instructor and anticipate what will be on the exams, so that they can study only what is pertinent. The result of this "getting smart" is generally a significant lowering of grades. If grades are important to you, you have to keep up your study program.

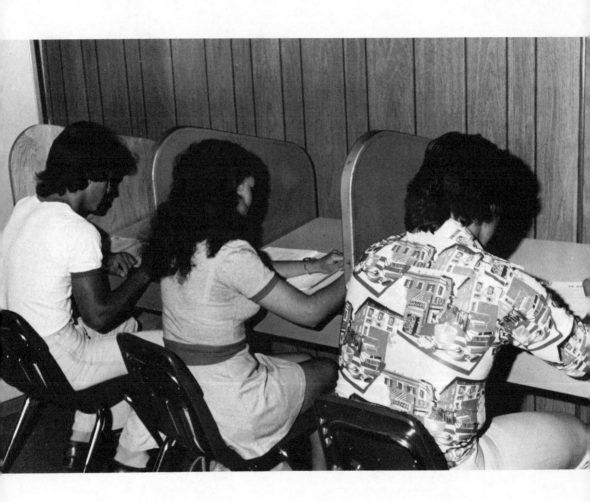

Chapter **6**

How to Take an Examination

We know that examinations are not perfect measuring devices of knowledge or ability. Nevertheless, your progress in your course work will be measured by examination. While imperfect, it is the best system we have.

You should look at the positive side. Treat the examination as a challenge, a chance to prove yourself. Obtaining good grades is ego gratifying. It will serve to increase your self-esteem. Unfortunately, all too often students view examinations negatively. They fear failure. This fear can lead to anxiety, which can interfere with your ability to answer the questions properly. If you have done your preparation work, there is nothing more you can do. Try to relax prior to your examination. One method that helps is to sit down, close your eyes, and take 20 deep breaths. Concentrate on holding each breath for five seconds, and count the number of breaths. You should find that this method will help calm your nerves, since the concentration required will take your mind off the examination. A good night's sleep will also help to reduce tension.

Most worry is unfounded; nevertheless, many students worry about "horror" exams where they can't answer a single question. While your examination may cover an area in which you are weak, if you have studied, very few if any of the questions will completely stump you. Remember that most people pass examinations.

If you mingle with other anxious students before an exam, you will heighten your own anxiety. Don't wait outside the door with the other students for the instructor to arrive. At this late time talking to others isn't likely to help, but it is likely to confuse you and increase your nervous tension. Nervous laughter, constant chatter, and frequent trips to the washroom are symptoms of pre-exam jitters.

While you should avoid the pre-exam socializing, you do want to be close to your examination room early so you can be sure of being on time. This protects you against unforeseen delays. Also, if you have to rush to get to your exam on time, you probably will arrive in an agitated state, and it will take some time to calm down.

When you get into the examination room, it is normally best to sit at your regular classroom seat if possible. Being in a very familiar position will help you to remain calm. After you start writing the examination, you will generally get so involved that any nervousness you may have will disappear.

Avoid sitting near friends. Friends can be distracting to you, and you want as few distractions as possible.

You should be well prepared with pens and pencils. If your examination room does not have a wall clock, a watch is essential. If your examination requires marking an IBM answer sheet, make sure you have the proper pencil (although this is usually furnished). Murphy's Law states that "whatever can go wrong will go wrong," so if you only have one pen, you can count on its running dry before you finish the exam.

If you have had to memorize a list of items and you are worried about it, you should write them down on the back of the exam or a scratch sheet as soon as the exam starts. By immediately writing them down, you will feel a sense of relief that you have rid yourself of a burden. After you start your examination, you normally will be calmer than when you are waiting to start.

Some students start writing at a rapid pace as soon as they can start. Don't do it. Read the instructions carefully as well as all of the essay questions. You should underline key words in the instructions and questions, such as "differentiate," "causes," "compare," "history," "evolution," "reasons," and "similarities." In this way you will be less likely to misinterpret the question. On essay questions you should pay particular attention to the verb. What are you being asked to do?

By pre-reading the examination, you avoid duplicating answers in the essays, and you will better understand what the instructor wants. You should also be on your guard for unusual directions. A careful reading of the instructions might show you are to answer three of the five essay questions given. If you had not paid attention to the directions, you might have given a rush treatment to all five questions rather than the detailed answers expected on just three questions.

Since you know how the examination is weighted as to points, you can allot your time based on the points given.

Also, since you have read all of the essay questions, as you write, ideas for other questions will come into your mind. You should jot these down immediately, as you might otherwise draw a blank when you get to the question. You should keep in mind that you should be answering the essay questions primarily with material learned during the course.

If you are not sure what an instruction means, then by all means, have your instructor clarify the meaning. You must know what is expected of you.

Your examination will be either objective or subjective o a combination of both.

Objective questions are true-false, multiple choice, matching, or completion. Generally, only one answer will be regarded as being correct. You are likely to have objective examinations in science and mathematics as well as in large classes where the sheer size of the class precludes the slow grading process of subjective tests.

Subjective examinations are essay examinations and call for your opinions and reasoning. Subjective examinations are used heavily in the humanities and social sciences.

Some instructors prefer objective examinations because of the ease in grading, and they feel the measurement is more meaningful, since personal bias is eliminated. Other instructors prefer subjective examinations because they feel this is the only way to measure the depth of your knowledge and understanding.

Before you start on the subjective questions, which will take a great deal of time, you should first complete the objective questions, which normally can be answered fairly rapidly. The fact that you have them complete will also help to calm your nerves. If you had completed the subjective questions first and found yourself running out of time, panic could easily set in, as you would be faced with a great number of objective questions and little time in which to complete them.

OBJECTIVE AND SUBJECTIVE EXAMINATIONS

From the instructions you will know whether the instructor is trying to discourage guessing. As an example, an instructor scoring a true-false exam might count the correct answers and then deduct from that score the number of wrong answers. The instructor in this case feels that by doing this he knows what percentage of the material you actually know. In this case you should still guess, since you should do 50 per cent even if you have no knowledge at all. Since you have studied and are prepared, you should expect to beat the mathematical 50-50 odds, which represent mere chance. In addition, the methods set forth in this chapter will enable you to consistently beat the odds of pure guessing even when you are being confronted with material for the first time.

You should read each question carefully and ask yourself, "What is really being asked?" Some instructors test you on the ability to read instructions and questions as well as the course material. When we read fast, we tend to read things as we expect them to be written rather than seeing what they actually say. As an example, most people have a positive outlook, but a question might be phrased as a negative, such as "the least important factor." A positive person could easily read this as the "*most* important factor" instead. Tests are not the place for speed reading. You must understand what is actually required.

OBJECTIVE EXAMS

On an objective test you should be on your guard for "mandatory words." These are words such as "always," "never," and "must." If you know that there are any exceptions to the statement at all and a question uses a mandatory word, then on a true-false exam the answer would be false. On a multiple choice question, the obvious answer might not be the correct one if there are exceptions to the statement. Questions containing mandatory words call for special care. If words such as "seldom," "normally," "generally," and "usually," are used, there can be exceptions to the question, and these few exceptions would not make the statement false.

You should keep in mind that even if part of a question is true, the correct answer is false if any part of the question is false. As an example, suppose the question were "Millard Fillmore was the 13th President of the United States (1840–43)." The answer would be false, since the years should be 1850–53.

Occasionally an instructor will use a double negative. If you remember that two negatives make one positive, you will have no trouble. As an example, "least likely not to . . ." would mean "most likely to . . . ."

For multiple choice questions you should be concerned with the best answer, not necessarily the correct answer. Don't mark down an answer until you have read all the choices. There may be several answers that are true, but one is more appropriate than the others. You might find that answers a and c are both correct, and answer d reads "both a and c." In this case d would be the correct answer.

If you don't know an answer, you can improve your odds at guessing by elimination. If you can eliminate one answer in a four-choice question as being obviously wrong, you have improved your guessing odds from one to four down to one to three. Of course, if you can eliminate three answers as being wrong, the remaining answer would have to be the correct one. Sometimes instructors throw in obviously wrong answers or even humorous wrong answers in order to complete a question. When they do this, they are really helping you by improving your odds of being right.

If you have absolutely no idea what the correct answer is to a true-false or multiple choice question, by following these simple directions you will be able to consistently beat the law of averages for guessing.

True-False Tests

1. If a question contains a mandatory word such as "always," "never," or "must," you should guess "false."

2. If a question contains a word such as "seldom," "normally," or "generally," where an exception would not alter the answer, guess "true."

3. If the statement is more specific than most, guess "true."

Multiple Choice Tests

1. If two answers contain a similar sounding word, such as "subordination," and "subrogation," choose one of these!

2. If two answers are almost identical except for a few words, choose one of these.

3. If one answer is unusually long or unusually short, choose that answer.

4. If two answers seem extreme, they should be eliminated and a guess made as to the remaining answers. As an example, if the answer is to be a number, and 3, 87, 89, and 1003 are the choices given, you should eliminate the 3 and the 1003 and take a guess at one of the two remaining choices.

5.   If the question is an incomplete sentence, and a particular answer when read with the question does not make a gramatically correct sentence, that answer should be eliminated and the guess made as to the others.

6.   If you are unable to eliminate any answer on a four-answer question, choose the third answer. Experience has shown that it has a better than 25 per cent chance of being the correct answer.

There is a difference of opinion about whether one should change answers once they have been written. The latest studies show that if, on reflection, you feel that an answer should be changed, you should change it. Of course, you should always change an answer when you realize you misread a question or another choice revealed the correct answer. Frequently you will find that questions unintentionally reveal the answers to other questions.

In taking an objective test, don't worry a question to death. That is, don't try to read too much into the question. Objective tests are recognition tests, so don't try to apply definitions not based on the course. Answer the questions based on your lectures and class reading, not based on additional knowledge you may have. Students who have been trained in law frequently have a great deal of difficulty with objective tests in that they read things into questions that the instructor never intended. Generally, your instructor will not be out to trick you, so you should not look for obscure meanings. A major fault with objective tests is that the more you know and the better you can reason things out, the more apt you are to read things into a question that were not intended by the instructor.

If a question requires a lengthy mathematical process in order to determine the correct answer you should try to eliminate obvious wrong answers and take a guess from the others. Put a note on your examination or scratch paper so you can work the problem out after you finish the examination if time permits. When questions are worth equal numbers of points, you must avoid spending a great deal of time on one or two questions. It is much better to have made a wrong guess than to have worked it out and be right and have also left 10 questions unanswered for lack of time.

On a multiple choice completion question, you should try to answer the question in your own words without looking at the answers. Then look at the answers, and if one approximates your answer, it is likely to be the correct one.

If you have a completion question in which you cannot remember the technical word, you should explain your answer in your own words. You may get some credit for this, and frequently by writing down your explanation, you will think of the term.

A matching question may have two columns in which you match a word or term in one column with a word or term in another. In answering a matching question, you are trying for the most appropriate answer. Don't assume that one answer can be used only once unless this is clearly stated in the instructions.

Never argue with the question. Accept it at face value. If the question is, "The moon is made of cheese and is 40 kilometers in diameter. A giant mouse can eat 100,000 cubic meters per second. How long will it take the mouse to consume the entire moon?" Don't say it is impossible. Either guess or calculate the answer. Don't waste valuable time being concerned that the question is not true.

Never add, delete, or change words in a question. If the question says "should," don't change it to "must." You must read questions the way they are written and not the way you would like them to be.

When you are answering on an IBM-type answer sheet, be careful that you are marking the correct question. Especially if you skip a question, it is possible to find yourself marking question 100 on the answer sheet when you are on question 99 of the test. This usually results in instant panic. Frequent checks will prevent this from happening.

Do not skip questions. If you are unsure, take a guess and indicate that it was a guess on your exam or scratch paper so you can review it later, if time permits. All too often students skip questions and turn in tests with questions unanswered.

When you use a separate answer sheet, try to keep the sheet to the right of your examination (if you are right-handed). In this manner you won't have to cross over your examination to mark the answer sheet, and you will be able to keep your place on the exam and proceed faster.

Most people, when marking on an IBM sheet, blacken in the proper area by going up and down, up and down, up and down. They may use six strokes with the pencil when one would do. These few additional seconds are worth a lot more in reading the questions than in having a nice dark mark. The computer will pick up one solid mark. You will also waste a lot of time if you find that you have to erase your nice dark mark. The computer normally is programmed to indicate a wrong answer if more than one answer is marked. Therefore, you must erase completely when changing answers.

In allocating your time for the examination, you should expect multiple choice questions to take about twice as long per question as true-false questions.

Subjective Exams

While objective examinations require recall, a subjective examination requires organization and frequently conclusions in addition to recall.

Many students, after reading the question, immediately start writing, without much of a plan. You should organize your answer before you start. A brief outline form scratched out is a point of beginning. The more points that an essay is worth, the more carefully you should organize your thoughts. Try to organize in a natural order. For history, a chronological order generally is applicable.

In answering subjective examination questions, go to the easiest question first. By completing an easy essay question, you will have more confidence because you have locked in points.

Essays

On many essay questions it is possible to write on and on, so you must watch the clock closely. Allot a specified time for each essay, and leave a cushion of time for a final check. When your time is up, finish up your conclusion and go to the next question.

Don't start your essay by repeating the question. This simply takes time and will not give you any additional points.

Your essay is really like a news story in that you will normally cover the topics who, what, where, when, and why, the last of which is your editorial opinion. Your essay should open with your thesis, which is the argument you intend to prove. Your conclusion should follow naturally from the facts. If there are other possible conclusions, these should also be covered.

Each paragraph should start with a strong sentence, explaining the main point of the paragraph. The rest of the paragraph should contain supporting data and examples.

Your essay must not stray from the question, so you must keep in mind what is being asked while you write.

Your essay should show, if applicable, relationships, sequence of events, relevant details, possible implications, causes, examples, and other appropriate issues.

The inclusion of a rough graph or table to prove a point will normally receive very favorable reaction from an instructor.

You should use the technical vocabulary of the course, and if you know applicable names and dates, you should use them.

Try to keep your sentences short and clear. Avoid complex sentence structure. You must keep in mind that someone has to read what you have written, so the more clearly you set forth your points, generally the better will be your grade.

Avoid making unsupported statements of "truths." Learn to give specific supporting examples. You should also back up your opnions. Don't just state that "Truman was a better president than Johnson." Support your judgment with facts.

You should number or letter your points, such as:

The following social factors led to the fall of Rome:
a.
b.
c.
d.

If you wish to call attention to a particular statement, you can underline it. Use of a yellow accent pen is very effective in making a point stand out. This is particularly good if your essay is poorly organized, and you failed to make the points in the proper order.

Short paragraphs with a line left between them will make reading a lot easier for your instructor.

If a definition is asked for, you should be complete and clear. Don't give too narrow a meaning.

Use the words of the lecturer if possible for definitions. Your own words may not be just as good when it comes to explaining or defining. While some teachers award high grades to dissenters who can justify their answers, other instructors punish dissent. If you wish to take a viewpoint contrary to that covered in class, you should be sure you justify it. Also, you should set forth the viewpoint of your instructor and its supporting data. This type of treatment will generally be regarded in a highly favorable light.

If you don't know the answer to an essay question, save it for last and hope the answer comes to you. If it doesn't and you still have no idea what to put down, don't leave it blank. Cover something related. When you are not sure, don't be too detailed; be general in your answer. Chances are you will get some credit, although not much, but this is better than zero points by leaving it unanswered. More important, once you start to write, frequently the answer will come to you. If you feel you have come up with the answer after wandering around the subject, you can underline the pertinent points or use a yellow accent pen. You want to be sure your instructor doesn't overlook the fact that you finally came up with a proper answer.

Don't attempt to pad or bulk out an answer that you feel is complete. Irrelevant verbal wanderings generally detract from what you have written.

Always leave a large space between essay questions. In this way you can fill it in later if time permits and if you think of additional points to be made.

Write on one side of the paper only so that you can fill in the other side if necessary later. This applies to use of exam "bluebooks."

Neatness does count on a subjective examination, as the instructor is going to be influenced negatively if he has difficulty interpreting what you have written.

Essays should be written in ink, since it makes reading a great deal easier. Objective portions of exams should be written in pencil so that erasures are possible. Avoid using a very hard lead that makes reading difficult. A No. 2 lead is recommended.

You needn't worry if some questions are longer than others. Every question will not take the same amount of time or words to answer.

Outlines.   Some students have learned to answer in an outline format. An example follows:

I.   Basic Premise: _____
     _____
     _____

II. Supporting Data
     A. _____
     B. _____
     C. _____
     D. _____
        1. _____
        2. _____
        3. _____
     E. _____

III.   Conclusion:_____
       _____
       _____

While an outline might appear very brief, it makes your knowledge (or lack of knowledge) stand out. If you have covered the points adequately with a sentence or two of explanation for each point and example, where applicable, the instructor will generally be highly favorable to the outline treatment. If you intend to use an outline format, it might be wise to ask your instructor his or her viewpoint on the use of outlines for subjective questions.

Avoid phonetic spelling and abbreviations. You might know that w/o means without and that ASA means American Society of Agronomists, but the instructor might not understand. When the instructor doesn't understand what you are saying, your grade will suffer.

Normally every test includes something you didn't contemplate being tested on. Treat the unexpected like any other question. Rarely does one question make the difference between success and failure.

AFTER THE EXAM

When you finish an examination, there is an urge to get out right away. You must fight this urge and use all of the time alloted. Proper use of this extra time can mean extra points. Go back to questions you marked down as being unsure of. When looking at a question that stopped you the first time, frequently the answer will now appear obvious. By rereading questions and answers you might find that you misread a question, or perhaps one of the other questions revealed the answer to you. Since we think much faster than we write, frequently we think we covered a point in an essay question, but we actually didn't. Check all computations and make sure decimal points are in the right place, which is the most common math error.

Don't look around when you finish to see how others are doing. All you should be interested in is yourself. In addition, looking around may give the instructor the idea that you are trying to cheat.

After you leave the class, make notes on the type of questions asked. Reconstruct the examination as best you can. Knowing the type of questions asked for the exam can help prepare you for future exams.

GRADES   The way your examination is graded will give you an indication of what the instructor was seeking. Frequently the instructor will discuss this in class. If you are in doubt even after the first examination, make an appointment with your instructor so that you can get the instructor's viewpoint.

Your examination results might show a need to change study and/or notetaking habits. Perhaps the instructor placed greater emphasis on outside reading than you anticipated. By studying the first examination, you can better know your instructor and what to expect for the next examination.

Each instructor grades subjective examinations a little differently, based on what the instructor feels is important. In a study made several years ago, a large number of English teachers graded the same term paper. Grades varied from A to D, with most of the grades in the B–C area. Obviously the paper satisfied the requirements of some instructors and failed to do so for others.

If you are able to obtain old tests that your particular instructor used in the past, you can learn a great deal about what to expect on exams and how the questions should be answered. Some fraternities and sororities keep old exam files that can give valuable insight as to what a particular instructor tends to emphasize. If your instructor is lazy, you might find questions from previous examinations repeated on your current examinations.

Besides the usual midterm and final examinations, your instructor might give section examinations and even unannounced or weekly quizzes. Generally unannounced or weekly quizzes are objective tests to make sure you are doing your required reading.

Some instructors give open-book examinations. For open-book exams you are generally expected to give citations and applicable quotes. Open-book exams are usually subjective and really require the same degree of preparation as a regular examination. In order to find items quickly, you can color tab your text and notebook on areas you expect to be covered. Because you can use up a lot of time looking for something, you are best off roughing out the answer and then looking as time allows for fill-in details.

Other instructors give take-home examinations. For a take-home examination you are expected to do a much better job than for an in-class exam. Your grading on this type of examination is liable to be much more critical. From a student standpoint, a take-home exam means a great deal of effort.

Besides examinations, you may be graded on workbooks, assignments turned in, term papers, class recitation, and oral reports. If you have been given an assigned seat, it is likely that class participation will be graded.

In class participation you should ask questions pertinent to the material. Do not ask personal questions or moot, unrelated questions. Always think out your comments fully and clearly.

Grading of examinations may be against a standard, such as below 70 is a D and over 92 an A. Grading could also be on a curve, where a certain percentage of the class gets an A, a percentage a B, etc. When the grading is on a curve, you are really competing against your fellow students and trying to beat them to obtain a place at the top of the class. When working against a standard, you are merely trying for a numerical score without regard to where anyone else is rated.

If you disagree with the grading or feel your interpretation of a question was correct, you should make an appointment to meet the instructor or see the instructor during office hours. Some instructors will change a grade if you can show you really understand the material; others will not.

If you have done your work, you need not have any fear of examinations.

NOTES

Chapter 7

How to Write a Term Paper

Some students try their best to avoid classes that require term papers and reports. They regard written reports as some form of medieval torture.

The reason these projects are assigned isn't that instructors are sadists. As an educated person in our society, you must learn to express your thoughts in writing. Written papers help you to develop this very important skill. A second reason is that it is an opportunity to learn outside of the classroom. Most of your formal education so far has been highly structured. That is, you have learned what your instructors have programmed you to learn. Written term papers train you to perform independent research and to evaluate facts for decision making. You are able to arrive at conclusions based solely on your own discoveries. In other words, term papers train you to think for yourself.

To accomplish these goals you do not require any natural writing ability. All it will take is organization and some time. A term paper is not only a great educational experience, it can actually be a lot of fun. It is also a relatively easy way to improve your grade.

CHOOSING A TOPIC

To start with, your instructor will normally give you some general guidelines for your paper. The general area to be covered will be given fairly early during the school term. Within this area you will have to choose a specific topic for your paper.

The topic you choose should really interest you. If you have real interest in the subject, you are going to be motivated in your work, and this is going to show in your results.

To help in choosing a specific topic, look at your text. What areas related to the subject of the paper really interest you? You can also use the library. Check in the periodical index under broad headings, and you will find many more specific headings. These should give you some ideas. The encyclopedias in your library may also help in providing you with an interesting subject or a different approach to an area.

You can go to both extremes in subject selection. It is important to avoid so broad an area that it cannot possibly be covered or so narrow an area that you will have great difficulty in obtaining sufficient data.

After you start writing you might determine that it would be best to limit the scope of your paper even more than you had originally contemplated.

A quick check of the card catalogs and periodical index in your library will indicate whether or not you have chosen a broad enough topic which offers enough information for your paper.

What you want to produce is an in-depth paper on a specific area. Your instructor will probably give you a required number of words or pages for the report. The purpose of this is to give you some idea of the level of effort expected. The instructor isn't going to count words, but he doesn't expect either a paper significantly shorter than the limit or a doctoral thesis that will be a burden to evaluate.

Talk to your friends about your choice of topics. Get opinions. You might come up with an entirely different point of view.

You should ask yourself:

1. Does my topic relate directly to the assignment?
2. Will my instructor feel that the topic is a worthwhile subject? You want to avoid papers on trivial matters.

If you are unsure about whether your subject is acceptable, you should discuss it with your instructor. Don't try to see the instructor before or after class when many students are making demands on his or her time. Check office hours or make an appointment to discuss your ideas. Never come to an instructor and say, "I don't know what to write." By doing this you have given yourself a very negative image in your instructor's eyes. Have some ideas and express them. Frequently an instructor will suggest modifications of one of your ideas. When an instructor gives input into the subject of selection of an individual paper, he or she will usually have a more positive attitude toward your paper. Of course, while showing that you are interested and concerned gives you a positive image with your instructor, you should not request help just to "make points."

After your term paper is assigned, you should set a time table such as the following:

Assume the paper is assigned September 12 and is due January 16.

Subject to be determined:	September 19
Research completed:	October 17
Rough draft:	October 24
Second draft:	November 14
Paper completed:	November 28

By starting to work immediately on assigned term papers, they can be done in a careful manner without the pressure of any deadlines. Many students wait until two weeks before they are due and then rush to work on their papers to the exclusion of their regular studies. They make the deadline, which is normally close to the date for their final exam, for which they find themselves wholly unprepared because they have been devoting time that should have been used for review to finishing their term paper. The hurried term paper is, at best, mediocre, and the final exam is usually no better.

It is much like the old story of the grasshopper and the ant. The ant, who plans for winter, which in your case is a due date and a final exam, is prepared, and the grasshopper, who chose to play during the fall, is frozen out.

RESEARCH

After you have chosen a topic, research is necessary. Making a brief outline of your paper as you think it should be will help you in doing your research and keep you on the right track.

An outline is merely an organizational tool that can help you to get your thoughts together and present them in a clear, concise order. This procedure is helpful not only for preparing material for class but also for study purposes. If you take the time to think about the relationships between topics before you try to present them, you can save yourself time and frustration.

The form of outlining is designed to indicate visually the logical relationships of ideas. Therefore, you should begin by stating your thesis or purpose. Then indicate all the major divisions of support with Roman numerals. These entries correspond to topic sentences within the proposed essay. More detailed support for the major divisions is indicated by capital letters, and even further support can be shown by numbered entries below the letters. For short essays, the major divisions and two or three subdivisions for each will probably constitute adequate planning.

Outlines may be of two types—topic outlines or sentence outlines. Topic outlines have just a few words or phrases to indicate the topics or subtopics that the essay covers. Topic outlines are sufficient for many short essays, especially for those that classify or present a process. Longer essays and those that will develop a thesis can often profit from a sentence outline. A sentence outline is one in which the writer sums up, in one sentence, what he wants to say about each topic or subtopic. The sentence outline forces the writer to think through exactly what he wants to say before beginning to write. By constructing a sentence outline, the writer discovers whether or not the thesis is supportable.

Consider the following example of a sentence outline:

Thesis: Newspapers provide their readers many helpful services.
I.   They inform on current events.
    A.   News stories present unbiased reporting of local and national occurrences.
    B.   Editorials present specific interpretations of important happenings.
II. They entertain their readers.
    A.   Personal columns provide advice and often amuse.
    B.   Movie and TV reviews provide interest in current entertainment.
    C.   Comic pages provide humorous views of life.
III. They provide comprehensive classified ads.
    A.   The classified ads list sources of useful services.
    B.   The classified ads list various items for sale.

A good starting point for your actual research is the encyclopedia. The library may also have specialized encyclopedias in your specific area. Be sure to check with the reference librarian; don't rely on finding everything yourself. In addition, the librarian can often show you specific applicable reference books.

In all of your research, you will have to take notes. Five by seven cards are probably the best way to take notes. Write on one side only so they can be spread out later. If more than one card is used for notes from one source, be sure to indicate this on each card. Indicate the source, author, publisher, data, and page. For periodicals (e.g., magazines, journals, newspapers), indicate title of periodical, volume, date, and page.

If you find illustration graphs or charts that you feel are valuable, you should make copies. Your library probably has a coin-operated copying machine.

Take notes in your own words. Don't copy what the author has said, unless you intend to quote, in which case you should indicate this with quotation marks.

Don't look only for authors who support your own point of view. Research other viewpoints. After checking your own text, the reference books, and encyclopedias, use the card files in the library. If you can't find much on your subject, use a broader heading. As an example, if you were doing research on placer gold mining, you could check gold mining, mining, geology, and possibly even books on hydraulics. Books on your subject often will refer to other sources in footnotes and bibliographies. These sources should also be checked.

Perhaps your best source for research will be the *Readers' Guide to Periodical Literature.* This should be used last, as the other areas are likely to give you a more complete foundation for this step of your research.

There are many volumes to *The Readers' Guide.* Start with the most current supplement and look up your subject area. It will probably be found under much the same headings as you used in the encyclopedias. From the unbound supplements, go back year by year, taking note of the magazines and pages you will need.

Your library may have some of the current magazines. Chances are you will have to go to microfilm for most of them. Your librarian will show you how to obtain the microfilm, or it may be available for ready access. The librarian will also show you how to use the viewer.

Now you simply find the desired articles, read them in the viewer, and take your notes. You should rapidly scan the articles on the viewer, looking for pertinent data. When you find it, read it carefully and take the necessary notes. All of us know how to scan a novel quickly to find the "spicy" parts. You are really using the same technique to find the data you are seeking.

Your library may not have as complete a microfilm library as you desire. By simply making telephone calls you can check with other libraries in your area to see whether they have microfilms of particular publications.

If you feel a particular publication will be desirable but you can't find a microfilm of it, you should write directly to the publisher and explain what you need. Frequently old issues are available, and if not, for a slight fee they will usually copy any desired article.

Libraries beyond your school library should be considered. Normally available books and reference works will differ. This is especially useful if there is a major municipal or another college or university library in the area.

Other sources of important data are the trade associations and organizations. You can use the *Encyclopedia of Business Information Sources* or the *Encyclopedia of Associations* (both published by Gale Research Corporation) to find applicable groups. Normally these associations have publications and data that can be beneficial.

The *New York Times Index* may also be a good source for your research. It is similar to the periodical index except that it covers the *New York Times* only. The *New York Times* is probably available on microfilm in your school library.

Libraries at colleges that have graduate schools are especially valuable for research in that they will have an index of doctoral theses. These theses, besides providing valuable material, will also give many more possible sources.

Don't tell your instructor that you can't find any material about your subject, because normally it will mean that you haven't really looked.

In performing your research, don't repeat similar information from different sources. This will simply give you too many 5 × 7 cards to work with. You should, however, write down the necessary information so that the source can be included in your bibliography. Look for new ideas or treatments as well as new material. Frequently you will have your own ideas about possible implications of your research. Put these ideas down on a card. Your mind is a source, the same as any book or article. The purpose of the research is to stimulate your own original thinking.

If your instructor has written about your subject, be sure to pay special attention to his or her articles or books and to indicate that you have done so by footnotes and/or your bibliography.

Since a basic purpose of your paper is independent study, most instructors will not allow team effort for papers. Even when your instructor allows it, collaborating on a paper is difficult and time-consuming, especially for people who are not used to working together. In addition, if the paper is a joint effort, your instructor will expect it to be a superior one.

You can readily see that research could be almost never-ending, and at some time you will have to say "enough." When you find that most of your research is simply rereading the same material in different words, you should consider calling a halt to your research.

Now that your research is done, you should start on a rough draft of your paper. The first step is to go through all of your note cards. Now make a new outline of your paper. After you have your outline, do your best to arrange your cards in accordance with the outline. Place a number on each card in sequence. This is to help you with footnotes. **THE ROUGH DRAFT**

Don't state, "This paper is submitted in accordance with the course requirements of . . .". That isn't necessary.

Unless a specific format is given, you should start your paper with a strong first statement that calls attention to the paper as well as sets forth your basic premise. For example:

> Harry Truman certainly wasn't any Messiah, but I am going to prove that he had an unparalleled insight into the problems facing America during his term in office.

> You wouldn't consciously eat garbage, but you might be better off if you did, compared to some of the "pure" food you will eat today.

> If you believe our national agricultural policy is based on sound economic policy that considers the needs of both the farmer and the consumer, you probably also believe in fairy tales.

Your introduction should continue with the purpose or basic proposition of your paper. State how and why your thesis will be accomplished. Don't be vague. You must clearly define the subject matter of your paper.

Now you should start with your 5 × 7 cards. You should write this rough draft rapidly, using the cards to spark ideas for you. You are not going to get by with one draft; your rough draft is a necessity. This will be your working tool to complete the paper.

Don't copy an author's words unless you want to quote. Direct quotations should be indicated. If you delete part of a quote that you feel is not material, use ellipsis points—three dots (. . .)—to show omission.

Be exact. Never misquote or change a quote around for your own benefit. If you use an author's ideas, give that person credit. Just put a number down referencing the appropriate card. Be clear and concise. Don't hunt for proper words on this first draft. You want to complete the draft in as short a time as possible, so try to clear a time period when you can devote most of a day to the task. If you believe an illustration or a graph is needed, make a note on your draft.

You should attempt to show implications and give opinions as you write. Make sure you consider other ideas, if applicable, and indicate why your approach is more realistic. Avoid emotional dialogue. Your paper is to be rational.

You may know that CADCD means California Association of Donkey Cart Drivers, but others may not be as well informed, so don't abbreviate. Proper spelling and grammar on the first draft are not your primary concerns, although these must be considered in your final paper. Avoid clichés such as "hard as nails," "smart as a fox," "smooth as silk."

You should avoid too many descriptive words, such as "He was a devious, evil, and cunning man of whom you could expect the utmost in chicanery." Save this type of writing for prose. You are writing a serious research paper.

After you have covered your facts, you should have a conclusion. Your conclusion should flow naturally from the supporting data. You should also consider further implications. Your conclusion should be an evaluation of the data presented. A term paper isn't simply a conglomeration of facts. It must include your personal ideas and conclusions.

When you feel the draft is finished, put it aside for a few days to a week. When you get back to your paper, frequently you will have many more ideas and possibly even a different point of view or emphasis for your paper.

Read through your rough draft first. On your rough draft you will find that paragraphs do not necessarily lead into each other. You will find that your organization can be improved. By cutting paragraphs out of your rough draft and putting them in a better order, using Scotch tape, you will soon have the paper in a more organized form. After you have reorganized your rough draft, and possibly made notes for changes, you should start writing your second draft.

On your second draft you can take your time. Make sure each paragraph reads properly. You should ask yourself whether or not you could make the paragraph clearer. Remember that this isn't ad copy, where you give a biased viewpoint. Make sure you are intellectually honest.

Each paragraph should start with a sentence setting forth the main point of the paragraph, and the rest of the paragraph should contain supporting detail. Besides making it easy to read, this helps your instructor in grading, since often, when a large number of papers are turned in, an instructor will read the first sentence of each paragraph and then go to the supporting detail only when of special interest. You should avoid overly long paragraphs. Short paragraphs make material easy to read.

Don't try to impress the instructor with your great learning. Use simple English except when dealing with technical terms, in which case always use them. If an explanation of a term is necessary, make sure it is included. Don't pad your paper with words to reach a desired number of pages. Padding usually detracts from what you are saying. If you are unsure, check your spelling. If you want to avoid using the same words many times, use a thesaurus (provides synonyms).

You should ask yourself whether or not your paper reflects the level of effort expected by the instructor. Ask yourself, "If I knew nothing about the subject, would I be led to the stated conclusions?" If not, you will need more justification. Ask yourself, "Does my paper appear to follow all specific instructions given?"

The second draft, in some instances, can be the final copy, but don't count on it. It may need corrections or a complete revision. Also, most people should have their papers typed. Handwritten papers are difficult and, in many cases, nearly impossible to read. On an examination, some sloppiness and grammatical errors are expected, but not on a term paper.

THE SECOND DRAFT

It is very difficult to proofread your own copy, as you can easily read things the way you think they read, not as they actually read. Therefore, have a friend proofread for continuity, clarity, grammar, spelling, and punctuation. After proofreading, you are probably ready for typing.

To start with, you should use 8½ × 11 inch white bond and preferably use pica type, rather than the smaller elite, as

THE FINAL DRAFT: FORM AND CONTENT

this makes reading much easier. Using fancy script type makes your term paper difficult to read.

You should include a title page. It should indicate the name of your school, the title of the article, the course name and number, as well as section number, instructor, and, of course, your name. As an example, your title page might appear as follows:

IS TRUTH FICTION?
by Tom Jones
Podunk City College
Logic 27a
Section 3
Instructor: Hubert Cummings

In the event you are given a cover page format, you should, of course, use it.

The title of your paper should, if possible, tell something about your paper, as well as catch the interest of the reader. Catchy titles sell commercial products and can help your paper.

Your final typed copy should have a two-inch lefthand margin, which will provide space for your instructor to comment. It should be double spaced, and all quotes should be indented or be set off by quotation marks. Quotations can be single spaced.

Number each page. It is best to indicate page 1 of 12, page 2 of 12, etc., and include your name at the top of each page. In this way, pages will not get lost or out of order.

Indicate footnotes with numbers. You can place an identifying number above and to the left of the first word of the paragraph as applicable. Use Arabic numbers, and number consecutively. You can place footnote references either at the bottom of each page or at the end of the paper. Usually it is preferred at the end.

Footnotes for books should show author, title, publisher, place of publication, year of publication, and page. The title should be underlined. A typical reference footnote would look like this:

[27]William Pivar, Getting Started (San Francisco, Ca.: Canfield Press, 1976), p. 93

For a magazine, your footnotes should be similar to the following:

Time—Mobile Homes in Trouble, Vol. XXV, Sept. 14, 1968, pp. 29-30

The term *ibid* can be used for a footnote identical to another one. If the page is different you can show this.

Details of proper organization and footnoting are available in *A Manual for the Writers of Term Papers, Theses and Dissertations* by Kate L. Turabian. This short book, published by the University of Chicago Press, is available in paperback.

In the event your school has a particular format for footnotes, or your instructor has indicated one, then, by all means, follow the instructions as given.

Mount any graphs or pictures firmly on 8½ × 11 inch paper. For more attractive lettering on graphs or title pages, you might consider press-on black letters, available at most stationery stores. Graphs should be done in black ink for clarity and possible reproduction.

At the end of your paper include a complete bibliography in alphabetical order. This bibliography can include sources not covered in footnotes.

To make your paper look better and to show your respect for what you have accomplished, you can back your paper with a blue legal backing, available at most stationers, or use a cardboard or plastic binding, available at your bookstore.

Don't try to plagiarize an article or use someone else's work as your own. Normally, an instructor will readily spot this by the organization and grammar. Also, don't invent sources, as many instructors will check on them when in doubt. It is common for instructors to come across papers that they know they have read before. It usually doesn't take too much effort to find out where, and the result is going to be failure. Even though many fraternities and sororities have term paper files, using them is like playing Russian roulette. Even if you are not caught, the grade you get may not really be that good.

OTHER PAPERS AND REPORTS

Besides the term or research paper, you may be assigned other reports or reviews. A report may be based on your own work, while a review is normally a critical evaluation of someone else's work.

For a book report, you should cover briefly what each chapter says. State the moral or messages the author is setting forth and what relevancy they have today. You should either agree or disagree with the author's ideas and give the reasons for your thoughts. In writing a book report, you should consider why the report was assigned.

Some instructors ask their students to make a separate oral report. Sometimes they are in connection with term papers. For an oral report, you should choose a subject in which you are interested. If you are interested, you are more likely to be enthusiastic in your presentation. You should start your report with a strong statement to get immediate attention. State your purpose, give supporting evidence, and then tie everything together with a conclusion. Really, this is just what you did in your written report.

The prospect of presenting an oral report makes many students nervous. Some students avoid classes for which oral reports are required. It is natural to be nervous when you know that you are going to be graded on a presentation and that a large number of people will be watching and listening to you. Once you start, your tension will lessen significantly and in many cases will disappear completely before the report is finished.

You should stand erect and practice before a mirror. Try to change your voice inflections. Try for eye contact with your audience. Use cue cards with key words or phrases to jog your memory. In this way, you won't have to read the report, and it will sound much more natural. Ask a friend to listen to you and evaluate your report. Often someone else can be a great help in pointing out areas that need clarification or areas of omission.

No matter what kind of report you give, you should learn to plan. The phrase, the early bird catches the worm, does apply, especially when the worm is really good grades.

NOTES

Chapter 8

Financing Your Education

The best things in life don't seem to be free when you start planning your finances for college. You will have to consider expenses such as:

Tuition
Room and board
Books
Transportation
Insurance
Clothes
Laundry and cleaning
Entertainment and recreation
Miscellaneous expenses

Ideally, financial planning for college should begin well before you enroll in college. Several years in advance is not too soon to start planning. Some schools are now charging over $6000 per year just for tuition and room and board. College costs, like everything else, have increased with inflation. Because of continuing cost increases, you can expect your expenses during your senior year to be significantly greater than freshman year expenses. For planning purposes you should estimate at least a six per cent increase in college costs each year.

The three basic solutions to any financial problem are:

1. Increase income
2. Lower expenses
3. Go into debt

All three aspects of solving your college financial needs will be covered.

INCREASING YOUR INCOME

One way to increase your income is to obtain a grant or scholarship. There are many thousands of scholarships available, ranging from very small amounts to full four year scholarships.

Information about the various scholarships that are available can be obtained from your guidance counselor or your financial aid office. In addition, scholarship information can be obtained in *How to Get Money for College* by Benjamin Fine and Sidney Eisenberg, *College Scholarship Guide* by Clarence E. Lovejoy and Theodore Jones, and *Lovejoy's College Guide.*

The American Legion publishes a booklet, "Need A Lift," which includes sources of loans and scholarships as well as career guidance information. The booklet is available from The American Legion Education and Scholarship Program, Americanism and Children and Youth Division, Indianapolis, Indiana 64206.

For minority students a booklet entitled "Going Right On" is available without charge from the College Entrance Examination Board, Publications Office, Box 592, Princeton, New Jersey 08540.

Most institutions require you to fill out either a PCS (Parent's Confidential Statement) or an FFS (Family Financial Statement) if you apply for financial aid. If you are self-supporting and have lived away from home at least a year and are not taken by your parents as a dependent for tax purposes, you will be required to fill out an SFS (Student Financial Statement). Information for these forms can be obtained from tax returns.

Since aid is generally based on need, a need analysis will be made by the school. Your need represents the difference between the amount the school feels will be your estimated expenses and what they feel, based on the financial reports, your family can contribute.

Many schools offer aid packages that are combinations of scholarships, grants, and loans. Often the scholarship consists of a reduction in tuition.

Most people have exaggerated ideas about the amount of scholarship money that is available. While you should definitely apply for every applicable scholarship, you should not base your decision to continue college solely on whether or not a scholarship is received. This is particularly true for students from middle income families. Today, most scholarships are based wholly or partially on financial need. If your parents are above the poverty level, it is difficult to obtain a substantial scholarship.

If you can show the need, one particular grant that is available is the Basic Educational Opportunity Grant. This is a federal aid program, and unlike a loan, it need not be paid back. Awards are based on need and are given to undergraduate students. The grants range from $50 to approximately $1000 and are intended to help meet educational costs. For applications and information about basic grants, see your financial aid office or write Basic Grants, Department of Health, Education and Welfare, Office of Education, Washington, DC 20202.

Students from extremely low-income families can also qualify for Supplemental Educational Opportunity Grants.

You should also talk to your instructors or advisors about available scholarships. Frequently they can help you to obtain one.

Having a full- or part-time job is the most common form of financial aid, although it is, of course, self-help. While some students have difficulty handling both school and a job, most students can at least work part-time and during summer vacation. An average student should be able to earn around $2000 per year without jeopardizing grades.

A job that relates directly to your career goal is, of course, the most desirable type. Chapter 10 deals in large part with obtaining this type of job. Because of the hours you have available to work, frequently it is not possible to obtain part-time work in your career field.

Jobs that are particularly attractive to students are waiter and waitress jobs in supper clubs. Advantages of these jobs are little training, hours compatible with school, far better than average income because of tips, and meals are generally included. In addition, restaurant jobs are available on a regular basis because of the high turnover of employees within the field. It may, however, be necessary to start at a position clearing tables or cleaning in order to work into a waiter or waitress position.

Other desirable jobs for students are car parking attendants at clubs and restaurants, as well as tutoring for college, high school, or grammar school students.

There are many jobs available that offer room and board, such as caring for a child as a babysitter or governess, housework, companion or aide for the elderly, chauffeur, gardener, houseboy. Because you might not be receiving a salary, these positions usually don't require many hours. They are also relatively easy to obtain, and an advertisement in a local paper is often effective. If you have difficulty, an employment service specializing in domestic workers should be able to help you.

Your student employment office, as well as your state employment office, can help you find a job; however, employers who contact these sources are frequently looking for cheap labor.

Some jobs, such as night desk clerk at a hotel or motel, or night watchman, pay very little but offer an opportunity to study when you are not busy.

If it is necessary to earn the maximum amount during the summer, you should consider work in the construction industry. If you can obtain one of these positions, you can expect to do well, because of high union wages. In recent years, women have been employed as flag persons on many road jobs.

One unusual problem for students has been that of getting too good a job. An excellent position can be a temptation to quit school. While it may not necessarily be a wrong decision, you should be certain it is well thought out and not simply used as an excuse to leave school.

Many schools have work experience programs. These programs are generally classified as parallel or alternate plans. In a parallel program, the student works while going to school at the same time. The student obtains some college credit for working and usually completes some work-related project.

In the alternate work experience program, the college usually finds one job site for two students, in their career field. The students then alternate between going to school full-time for a term and working full-time for a term. While it takes twice as long to finish school under the alternate program, the student is able to save enough during each work period to pay the expenses for the next school period. The work experience administrator at your school may be able to place you in a position for either the parallel or the alternate program.

You can obtain $100 every month for your junior and senior years while attending college by joining the Army, Air Force, or Navy ROTC. You will also be paid for summer training. In addition, scholarships that pay for books, tuition, and other purely educational expenses are available. As an aviation reserve officer candidate, you will actually start flight training at government expense while attending college. This training is offered at regular civilian flight schools.

The U.S. Marine Corps has a Platoon Leaders class. Unlike ROTC, your school need not have ROTC training to be eligible. All training takes place during two six-week summer courses, but you also get $100 per month for your junior and senior years. Another advantage of the Platoon Leaders class is that your time in school counts as service time for pay purposes.

Even if you do not plan on a military career, the financial aid can help you finish school. Of course, you will have a military obligation. Details of these programs are available from any military recruitment office or your campus ROTC officer, if you have one.

You should sit down with your parents and decide what financial commitment they can make. They should have a realistic idea of the total educational costs based on present and anticipated expenses. In the event that they decide that they can pick up all the expenses, you should consider yourself lucky. At the other extreme, they may decide they can't help you at all, in which case you will be on your own. They may decide they can pay tuition only, or tuition and dormitory room and board costs, or simply a given amount of money per year. Your parents will have to analyze their ability to help based on their income, other financial commitments, and expenses and savings.

A form of savings frequently overlooked by parents is their life insurance policies. It is possible to borrow on these policies at comparatively low interest rates. Life insurance has sent thousands of students through college. Sometimes parents obtain loans from banks, credit unions, or even relatives, to finance their children's education.

Because of inflation, if your parents own their home, chances are they now have a substantial equity. Refinancing or taking a second mortgage can be a means of raising money.

The final decision should be based on realistic cost estimates and careful evaluation of your parents' financial status. Frequently in large families, even those with substantial incomes, the parents' aid to each child will, by necessity, be limited.

Marriage before graduation frequently increases financial problems. Some parents will use it as an excuse to stop or reduce the aid to a son or daughter. They may say, "If you're old enough to marry, then you're old enough to take care of yourself." By talking to both sets of parents in advance, frequently it is possible to continue the education of both you and your spouse.

If one of your parents is receiving Social Security benefits or is deceased but was covered by Social Security, you are probably eligible for Social Security educational benefits. To receive these benefits you must be a full-time student. Check with your local Social Security office as to your eligibility. The War Orphans Educational Act provides benefits for children of totally disabled veterans and children whose parent died from service-connected disability.

Some students decide to take a year or a semester off to work in order to save money. Again, this is excellent—if the student returns. Often the thought of going back to school and having to pinch pennies again causes people to abandon the idea of returning to school.

By stretching college out from four years to five or even six years, it is possible to hold a full-time job and take a lighter schedule. Many people complete their education in this manner, although in working full-time there can be many pressures to quit school. Evening classes after a full day's work get to be quite a drag year after year. What frequently happens is the night student takes a breather for one semester and never returns.

LOWERING YOUR EXPENSES

One way to lower expenses is to compact your school into a shorter period of time. This can be done by carrying overloads and/or attending summer sessions. It is possible to complete a four-year degree in three years or even less.

In some families where there are several children close in age, the children take turns going to college, with the parents supplying support to only one child at a time. Many husbands and wives take turns, with the husbands getting the degree while the wife works, and then working in turn while the wife finishes school.

Ben Franklin was right when he said that "a penny saved is a penny earned." Cutting school expenses by $1000 per year is the equivalent of earning an additional $1000. One way *not* to save money is by sharing books. Grades are too important to have to rely on the availability of a shared book.

By buying used textbooks directly from other students, you can save significantly on your book expenses. Your school bulletin boards usually list many used books for sale.

You can often buy used books at half price. In addition, many bookstores in college areas, as well as college bookstores, carry used texts at approximately 1/3 off the new price. Because of the demand for used books, you should try to buy them as soon as you know you are registered in a class. Make sure the used book you are buying is both the proper text and the current edition for the required class.

Clothing can be a big expense or a minor one, whatever you want to make it. Today we have much more casual student fashions. You can outfit yourself satisfactorily from Brooks Brothers on the one hand or the Salvation Army store on the other. Clothing expenses are variable expenses, and can generally be cut. Because styles vary at different schools, it is recommended that you not buy an extensive wardrobe prior to attending college. Freshmen and sophomores tend to be the most fashion conscious students. Juniors, seniors, and graduate students tend to show more individuality in dress.

While dues and fees for various organizations and extracurricular activities can be eliminated, such activities are very important in making you a whole person. Your future employers are going to be very interested in your extracurricular activities. Those expenses should only be pared as a last resort.

Room and board is a major area of expense. If your school maintains dormitories, you will find that, generally, you could not obtain as reasonable a cost on the local economy if you were by yourself. Occasionally, by sharing an apartment with several students, you can obtain lower overall costs.

A decision about where to live is, of course, going to affect your expense. Rent is a variable cost, and savings are possible. A room can usually be rented for much less than an apartment. With a room you will have to buy meals as opposed to an apartment, where you can cook. Generally, for one person an apartment is more costly. Sharing apartments can reduce costs significantly.

While food costs can be cut, you should keep in mind that going to school is hard work, and you must keep yourself physically fit. A breakfast including milk and eggs will provide you with energy and "brain power" to start the day. You should strive for a well-balanced diet, including meat, vegetables, and fruit. Fad diets should be avoided, as they generally lack basic nutritional requirements for maintenance of good health.

Of course, if you can live at home throughout your college career, you will have significantly reduced costs. Sometimes it is also possible to live with relatives in the area.

Many students work for their meals at sorority or fraternity houses or at local restaurants. Frequently you can arrange to work one hour in exchange for a meal.

Laundry and cleaning expenses can be cut down by use of laundromats and cleaning machines. Many students keep a travel iron to touch up and keep their wardrobe in good shape.

Today one of your largest expenses will be your car. Often students, when confronted with a choice of continuing school or keeping their car, choose their car instead of their education. Our society places a great deal of importance on owning a car, and the need for private transportation is very important to many people. Ideally, you should decide whether owning a car is absolutely essential. Alternatives are public transportation, motorcycles, bicycles, feet, and friends with cars. Car repairs, payments, parking fees, oil and gas, and insurance can and frequently do exceed room and board expenses. Often a car is a luxury that can be put off. It is frequently more economical to rent a car when one is absolutely essential than to endure all the expenses of ownership.

You should, whenever possible, avoid long-term financial obligations. Buying things on installment credit, even if it only means a few dollars per month, can turn into a burden when you find yourself counting pennies.

You should avoid long-term commitments such as apartment leases. It might seem like a good idea for you and two other students to sign a one-year lease for an apartment, but you might find yourself obligated for the entire rent should you lose your roommates. Whenever possible a month-to-month rental is preferable.

You should avoid signing any document that can possibly lead to future financial obligations. As an example, you should never cosign for anyone else on a loan unless you are able and willing to pay that person's debt. All too often the cosigner ends up paying.

Some additional ways to save money are:

1. Make out a budget. Study your checkbook to get an idea of where your money goes. Strive to live within the budget.

2. Don't change your spending habits on pay day or whenever you receive money. Frequently students tend to purchase more non-necessities during these periods.

3. Carry only a minimum amount of cash with you. This reduces your ability to spend impulsively for non-necessities.

4. Use checks only for paying bills or emergency use. Because checks are not like real money to many people, they tend to spend more with checks than they would even if they had the cash with them.

5. Do not use credit cards. They are an easy way to upset your budget. People spend more freely with credit cards than they do with cash.

6. Make a shopping list of what you need. Buy only what is on the list. This is to avoid impulse spending for wants rather than needs.

7. Avoid rationalizing small expenses with "it's only a dollar" or "for five dollars you can't go wrong." Ask yourself, "What would happen if I didn't buy?"

LOANS

The third alternative to financial problems is to go into debt.

While you might have difficulty borrowing money, your parents, by cosigning, can help you to borrow money even if they are unable to help you directly.

Check with your financial aids office. Many schools have students loan funds for both regular aid and emergency aid. In addition, many states provide special student loan programs.

The federal government provides national direct student loans for up to $2500 each year. These loans are based on need, so parent and student incomes are a major factor. In addition, Federal Insured Student loans from local lenders are also available. The borrower can borrow up to $2500 per year. Generally, student loans do not have to be paid back until after the borrower ceases to be a student (usually after graduation).

At one time the reason many students went to college was strictly financial. Today, the high cost of college and higher blue collar wages have decreased the economic advantage significantly. The reasons that you are in college today should be because education can make you a happier, more productive person. It can help you in being able to realize your potential. Your education will cost you time and money. If you are willing to make the necessary sacrifice, you can succeed.

NOTES

Chapter 9

Adjustment to the College Environment

College will offer you many new opportunities. You will meet new and interesting people with different ideas and values. You will hear new points of view from teachers and new friends. You will have the opportunity to make decisions. Intellectual challenges not present in high school or in jobs are before you.

There is a great deal of hustle and bustle at college. There is always something happening. You can go in many different directions or you can stay put. You don't have to get involved in everything right away. Take the time to pick the groups you are interested in. After making decisions, don't wait to be invited; express your interest. You can gain a great deal from extracurricular activities. They go a long way in the development of interpersonal skills.

Don't limit yourself to one group of friends who think as you do. You have an opportunity to form lasting friendships with people having diverse viewpoints. Both formal and informal groups can be very meaningful. They also help to fulfill your human needs of recognition and belonging.

Future prospective employers will be interested in the groups you belonged to at college. If you didn't belong to any groups, they might assume that you had an adjustment problem, or they might consider you dull. Holding office in a club or organization will be regarded as an indication of leadership ability.

Sororities, fraternities, and other social clubs have lost much of their former importance on campus. Normally, social activities are of primary importance to these groups.

These groups, however, can be particularly helpful to students who have difficulty relating well to others.

Some students adopt "far out" ideas to get attention. As members of an unusual group, they are able to get status and recognition. Often this type of group attracts "loners," those who normally have trouble relating to their peers.

Some religious cults recruit this type of student today. By being accepted into the group, the student gets recognition. Some students tend to become fanatical in allegiance. Certain pseudoreligious groups today utilize modern brainwashing techniques. Students who join such a cult may become alienated from all except other members of the religious group, and their personal goals may become subservient to the goals of the cult.

Religion can help you. It can give you courage and strengthen your relationship with God. Don't be ashamed of being a religious person. College is not filled with a bunch of agnostics. But before you get involved with any group, be sure you understand the group fully and what your involvement will entail.

The peer group or groups with which you become involved at school are going to determine much of your own action.

ROOMMATES

College may be the first time you have had a roommate other than a family member. This can be an opportunity to develop your interpersonal skills. If you have the opportunity to choose a roommate, look for someone with the same values, but not necessarily the same interests. To live in harmony with someone else requires some adjustment in your life style. This is true for roommates, lovers, and spouses. The following simple rules of living will help you get along with your roommate as well as with others. They apply to college and life in general.

Respect the privacy of your roommate. Don't pry into personal affairs. If your roommate wants you to know, he or she will tell you.

Respect also your roommate's social privacy. Just as you have friends, so does your roommate. Don't become an uninvited tagalong.

Don't borrow your roommate's possessions or use his or her toiletries without permission. Often it is these little annoyances that are the most irritating.

Treat your roommate as an equal. At home you may have ordered younger brothers and sisters around, but don't try to give orders to your roommate.

Respond in a positive way to the achievements and possessions of your roommate. Some people try to build themselves up by belittling others.

When you do have an argument, try to be fair and to treat your roommate with respect. Remember that there are always at least two sides to an argument.

Try to foster a considerate, nonthreatening social interaction. Avoid competing for the same dates or positions whenever alternatives are available.

Be modest about your possessions and those of your family.

If you discuss your roommate with other people, be fair. Try to say only the kinds of things you would want your roommate to say about you.

If it is necessary for you to be critical of an action of your roommate, learn to criticize in a positive way. You must allow people to keep their self-respect.

Show that you are interested in your roommate as a person.

Learn to listen to your roommate. Many people tend to hear what they want to hear, rather than what is being said.

If you are having problems with your roommate, wait until you are both calm before discussing them. Avoid trying to solve problems when either of you is in an emotional state.

While your roommate isn't going to be perfect, neither are you. But your roommate is a human being with feelings that you should respect.

STRESSES OF COLLEGE LIFE

If you are shy and have serious problems in relating with others, you should seek help. Your counselor will be able to direct you to psychological counseling.

At some time or another you are going to feel lonely. It is a normal feeling that everyone experiences at some time. You can have this feeling even in the midst of a crowd. One common cure for loneliness is to get involved in some outside activity.

College has built-in stresses. We start with competition for grades; couple this with the importance of success, and it is clear that this is a point in your life at which you are likely to be highly emotional.

Severe depression may be caused by poor grades, things not working out as planned, health worries, a broken romance, sexual hangups, loneliness, arguments, parental pressures, feelings of inadequacy, worry over the state of the world, and even fear of things that just might happen but probably won't. Often the problem can be cumulative, the result of many small things, and the student may suffer depression without really being sure of the reason.

SUICIDE

Suicide is the second leading cause of student deaths (accidents are first). Suicide sometimes seems a very simple solution to a difficult or stressful situation. There may even be a desire to "get even." A depressed person may say to himself, "They'll be sorry they treated me that way," or "I'll show them." Suicide thus is thought of as a weapon against others, but of course such deaths are tragedies, and the suffering they cause profits no one.

Most suicides are not successful, largely because people who contemplate suicide don't really want to die. What they really want is for someone to care about them, to know of their unhappiness. This is evidenced by the fact that many suicides call friends or relatives to tell them that they are going to kill themselves. Such an action should be regarded as a cry for help.

Anxieties, coupled with lack of sleep, are mental danger signals. If a student talks about death or suicide while under pressure, someone should remain with the student. Another sign of emotional upset may be lying down during the day and staring at the ceiling in a student who normally does not lie down during the day. If you are worried about your mental state, or that of a friend, you should seek aid. Avoid self-help type encounter groups that are not under expert direction. These sessions, in which everyone says what he or she really thinks, can be extremely ego damaging if not run properly.

Sports participation or other heavy physical activities offer you a relief valve for your emotions. Contact sports especially can be helpful.

Another outlet for emotional relief is simply to talk your problems out with a friend. Don't bottle up your worries or feelings. Frequently when you verbalize a problem, it doesn't seem as insurmountable. Many problems are actually imaginary but nevertheless seem real to the person involved.

Men have been taught since childhood that showing emotions is for girls and is not manly. They "keep a stiff upper lip'' and bottle things within themselves. This attitude frequently leads to serious emotional problems.

Often during the second year in college, everything seems to go wrong. These sophomore problems are caused by a number of factors. Upon getting good grades the first year, many students ease off a little, which often is too much. The overconfidence of a ''this isn't so bad'' attitude can result in disastrous grades. Also, by the second year the student is starting to get involved in outside activities, which can result in neglect of education. To some students, the extracurricular activities become more important than education. You should be aware of this ''Sophomore Trap.''

"Sophomore Trap"

At this stage in your life, many of your problems will be sex-related. Sexual feelings are natural. Not so many years ago most people wouldn't discuss sexual matters even with their own spouses. Today, people are more apt to talk about sex openly.

LOVE AND SEX

We, as human beings, are naturally gregarious. That is, we like other people. We want to feel wanted by others. We need recognition by others. We have the desire to make strong friendships. "Meaningful relationship" is the term frequently used for this type of attachment.

Dating during college should not be a game of chess, with each party looking for an advantage. It should be mutually beneficial and enjoyable. A healthy attitude can build both egos. Dating should be a comfortable relationship, not a win-lose competition. Don't build relationships into something they are not. Let them develop on their own. Unrealistic expectations can lead to severe letdowns.

Despite a great deal of open talk about sex, the dual standards for men and women still exist. Some men still believe in one standard for the women they date and another standard for their mothers, sisters, and the woman they expect to marry.

Many students are in love with love. That is, they want to be in love so much that they tell themselves they are in love. Sex should not be confused with love. Love is an emotion, and although words cannot adequately describe emotions, it can be said that when you love someone your center of interest transfers from yourself to another, who replaces you as being number one in your thoughts and future.

In college many students seek casual sexual relationships. They feel that if both parties are mature, they can have a convenient relationship without becoming emotionally involved. However, you should realize that the desire not to become emotionally involved doesn't mean that you won't. A relationship can seldom be ended without some emotional scars.

We are finding more open, nonconforming sexual relationships (such as bisexuality or homosexuality) at college. Some of these relationships are not just open but are practically advertised, whereas in the past they would have been kept highly secret. You should consider the effect of such relationships on your family and upon your partner's family.

Largely because of lack of understanding, many people have sexual hangups. That is, they have mixed feelings, fantasies, and fears which they feel are abnormal. Such fantasies and thoughts, although they may be frightening to you, are perfectly normal. Sexual problems should be talked out with a counselor.

VENEREAL DISEASE

Venereal disease has increased at an alarming rate. One of the problems has been that "the pill" has replaced other forms of contraception. Some of the new varieties of disease are resistant to penicillin and are not easily cured.

The two basic types of venereal disease are syphilis and gonorrhea. In syphilis, the first symptom is a sore or chancre (which often is not detected in women). Because the symptom disappears does not mean you are well, since syphilis does not go away unless treated. If left untreated, syphilis can lead to brain damage, insanity, damage to other organs, paralysis, and death. Gonorrhea, also known as "clap," normally has an initial symptom of burning during urination, although 80 per cent of women with gonorrhea have no symptoms. Gonorrhea, if untreated, can result in sterility, as well as heart and brain damage. In addition, women with gonorrhea can cause blindness in their children. Should you have any symptoms of venereal disease, you have a duty to notify your partner at once. The only sure way to know whether you are infected is a physical examination. If you want more information, check with your college medical office or your own physician.

Pregnancy still happens at college, despite the ready availability of contraceptives, primarily because sex isn't always planned, and contraceptives are not always absolute protection. Generally, marriages entered into primarily because of pregnancy have two strikes against them. Considering the fact that approximately half of all marriages end in divorce, the chances of a forced marriage succeeding are not very good.

Often students marry for marriage's sake. Everyone else is getting married, and the students decide it isn't such a bad idea. The party they are dating at the time becomes the likely candidate. Marrying just to get married or to escape parental control or some other problem generally will mean real trouble later on.

Drug problems exist at college, just as they do elsewhere. For basic drug information, see the Appendix. For drug problems, your counselor can direct you to professional help.

DRUGS

At one time you knew that your parents could protect you and solve all your problems. You regarded them as very special people. As you matured, you discovered that your parents are not any different from other people. They have the same problems and feelings as everyone else. When an image is shattered, people tend to go to the other extreme. Upon seeing their parents' imperfections for the first time, adolescents may feel that their parents have no good qualities at all. You might feel that they interfere with your life. When your parents force something on you or tell you that you cannot do something, you might very well do the opposite if you have the chance. This is not so much a rejection of the ideas of your parents; it is more an act of rebellion. It applies to sex, drinking, and many other actions.

GETTING ALONG WITH YOUR PARENTS

The fact that your parents still look upon you as a child when you want to be regarded as an equal often precipitates conflict. Parental conflict also results because you may be dependent on your parents for most of your needs, but you resent this dependency. Your parents might feel that as long as they are paying the bills, you should do what they say.

Understanding your parents is a two-way street. Your parents are under stress, just as you are. Getting along under stress can be difficult. Your parents may have financial stress or a fear of failing. If you fail, they may feel they have failed. They worry about what can happen to you. Some parents, although financially successful, regard themselves as failures for one reason or another. They might fear that you will end up like them. They might desire to live vicariously through you and want you to have and do the things they did not have or do.

Your parents received no special training in how to be parents. Many times they did not know whether to be tough or lenient, and they may have been inconsistent in their treatment of you. Their feelings toward you may have resulted in family conflict. They are afraid of doing the wrong thing but are unsure of what is right.

You should regard your parents as beautiful people. They have feelings. Their egos need building up just as yours does. Give them words of encouragement. Make them feel successful. Allow for their mistakes. Even if you know they are mistaken, remember that they are trying to help you.

Make the most of your college experience. It can make you into a more sensitive and understanding human being as well as provide new horizons of knowledge. Your college experience can go a long way toward making the rest of your life more rewarding.

NOTES

Chapter 10

Employment During and After College

Unless you are going to spend your life as one of the idle rich or the unemployed poor, you can expect to spend the greater portion of your life gainfully employed. Even women who as girls fantasized about staying home and playing house after marriage now look forward to careers.

The result of the economics of our modern society as well as an increasing realization that marriage is made up of two equal partners is that women, both single and married, are becoming accepted as a natural and permanent part of our work force.

Working within your career area prior to graduation will make you a far more valuable employee than a graduate with no specific experience. This experience will give you a great deal of leverage in finding permanent career employment, especially if there should be a tight job market when you graduate. In addition, having direct experience will frequently allow you to negotiate a higher starting salary than someone with no directly related work experience would expect to get. As an example, assume your career goal is to work with emotionally disturbed children, and you are studying psychology. If you obtained summer work in a clinic or summer camp dealing with these children, you would find it very valuable in terms of your career as well as personally rewarding.

Direct job experience during college also offers several other advantages. Actually, working on a job will give you valuable insight as to curriculum planning. You might see the need to take courses other than those originally planned or even to modify or change the emphasis of your career program. Working within a career area can also reveal whether you have been correct in your career choice. Naturally, if you are going to change career goals, the sooner in your educational program that you do so, the easier it will be.

Many students who obtain summer employment and prove themselves dedicated employees end up being offered full-time jobs. At one university that has a program for providing jobs directly related to the student's career field over 50 per cent of the students receive full-time job offers from these summer jobs.

Whether or not you work during college, chances are you are going to have to obtain employment in the future. All too often, highly trained students graduate and then feel they are lost. They really have no idea as to what to do next. Until this point they had counselors and instructors to give them guidance. Now they feel they are being set loose in a sink-or-swim situation.

Just as it is possible to plan an education to fulfill your individual needs, you can plan to obtain employment based on those same needs. If you wish to supplement your education with directly related work experience during college, your job search should really begin shortly after you start college. If you have a career goal, or even areas that interest you, then you are ready for the first step, which is to analyze the market.

Make a list of firms in the area that can utilize your training. By going through the yellow pages of the phone book, you will find firms you never knew existed. Your school or public library will have phone books from other areas. They will also have *Moody's Industrials, Dun and Bradstreet* and *Thomas' Register.* Besides listing firms, these books give valuable information about them. From these sources you can easily obtain information about firms nationwide that can use the training you expect to have. The *Encyclopedia of Business Information Sources,* published by Gale Research Company, lists trade and professional organizations, and the *Encyclopedia of Associations,* also published by Gale Research Company, lists trade, business, government, scientific, educational, cultural, and labor associations and their publications. By writing to the applicable associations, you can get information about its members both locally and nationally. Also, by obtaining their publications you will get specific information about developments within your career field, as well as data about specific firms. Check with the U.S. Civil Service. Many government agencies have summer intern programs. Uncle Sam is, of course, our largest employer. Don't overlook the student employment office on campus. They might have a job that fits right in with your career plan.

Your instructors, as well as the campus placement office, can probably supply you with the names of firms that have hired recent graduates within your area of interest.

The purpose of this preliminary search for job sites is to find summer employment, and possibly even part-time employment during the school year, within a career area that interests you.

After your initial research, you should list all the firms you are interested in. For firms within your geographical area, you will want to present yourself in person for an interview. For firms outside the area, you will usually have to rely on letters or telephone calls, because of the time and cost of traveling. Before you personally contact a local firm, you should obtain as much information about the firm as possible. Among sources of information are the local chamber of commerce, friends who might know an employee, and local businesses in the area. You want to know as much as possible about the firm. If you can't find the name of the manager of the firm or of the division in which you are interested, simply call and ask the secretary the name of the appropriate manager.

You should now call the manager, and your conversation should be similar to the following:

THE INITIAL INTERVIEW: SUMMER AND PART-TIME JOBS

"Mr. Thomas, my name is Fred Brown, and I am an engineering student at State College. I plan to specialize in stress analysis. I'd like to stop by and talk to you for just a few minutes. Would Friday at two o'clock be convenient for you?"

You are not telling Mr. Thomas what you want, only that you are a student in a field in which he is very interested. Most people enjoy talking to students in their career area. By setting a time you make it very easy for Mr. Thomas to say yes. If Mr. Thomas can't make it at two o'clock, he will probably suggest another time when it will be convenient for you to stop by. Don't schedule an appointment for Monday morning, since in most firms it is one of the busiest times.

When you go to an interview, keep in mind that the people doing the interviewing are generally older and more conservative than the people being interviewd. You should, therefore, dress accordingly. Exceptions are fields such as advertising, art, and entertainment, where more modern styles are the norm. You should be dressed and groomed in a way that you feel the person interviewing you would expect the model student to appear. Regardless of how you dress, you should appear clean and neat. Don't chew gum or smoke. Avoid excessive perfumes, scented deodorants, or aftershave lotions. Use of a breath freshener is a good idea. Walk erect, and greet the person you wish to see with a firm handshake. Make sure your hand is dry, as a clammy hand turns people off. You should also make sure that you pronounce the interviewer's name correctly. Although at this time, the person doesn't know that he is to become an interviewer, you should explain your career goals to him. These should, of course, fit into what the firm is doing. You should tell your interviewer what courses you have taken and are taking.

Explain that you are interested in what this firm is doing, and why, and that you would like to have work experience there for the summer (or possibly part-time and summer, if applicable). You are really saying, "I know what you are doing, I am interested in what you are doing, and I would like to play a part in what you are doing."

Chances are that this approach will be positively received. Keep in mind that you are talking to a manager about a position that probably doesn't exist. If you have sold yourself, there is a good possibility that a job will be created for you. This is especially true of summer jobs, when vacations result in many scheduling problems. Actually, if you are hired because of vacation problems, the chances are you will be exposed to various work situations, which will greatly enhance the value of your work experience.

If the interviewer is interested, but doesn't really offer you a position, ask for a job. As an example:

"I believe that I've shown you that I'm an energetic and dedicated student. Would you like me to work for you this summer?"

By a few words, you have made it easy for the employer to make an immediate decision.

Nothing has been mentioned about personnel offices. Generally, they should be avoided for summer jobs, because unless they actually had an opening, the result would be a polite letter stating that they are not hiring. Normally, the personnel office is not likely to set up a nonexistent summer position, whereas a midlevel manager could do so.

If you do not obtain a job, you haven't wasted the interview. You can use the opportunity to obtain additional career guidance. People are generally flattered when you ask them for guidance, and they usually will try to help you. You can ask for suggestions about elective courses you might take and obtain information about further specialization and future employment prospects. You should also ask if they can suggest any other firm in the field that could use someone with your career interest for summer employment. If a suggestion is made, find out who specifically to contact. You would then be able to say, "Mr. Thomas of Thomas and Associates suggested I contact you." This personal approach generally has a positive effect.

Never leave an unsuccessful job interview without leaving a résumé. An example of a simple résumé is shown in the box.

RÉSUMÉ

Résumé: Fred Brown
1476 Maple Lane
College City, Mo. 52816
(726) 589-4168

Objective: Summer employment with an engineering group involved in stress analysis. I would like experience that will reinforce my educational goal as a stress analysis engineer.

Education: Currently completing my freshman year at State College, enrolled in mechanical engineering.

At Center City High School I graduated 12th in my class of 189 students. In high school I took math courses through trigonometry, as well as three years of mechanical drawing.

Previous Employment: I have worked part-time through high school as a newsboy and as a boxboy for the Center City Market.

Organizations and Awards: Member of Alpha Tau Alpha student engineering fraternity, Boy Scout (Life Scout), Vice President of Student Council in high school, winner of Hiram Chambers Scholarship Award, Varsity letter in baseball.

Personal Data: Age: 19
          Height: 5'11"; Weight: 165 lb.
          Health: Excellent

References will be supplied upon request.

The résumé, whenever possible, should be limited to one page. It should contain identifying data; otherwise, an employer may forget to whom it belongs and it will be worthless. worthless.

The Objective sets forth, in a clear fashion, what you are looking for. It also gives you an opportunity to sell yourself.

Your Education block should show directly related experience. If you ranked high in high school, this should be indicated.

The purpose of showing previous employment is to show that you are a person who isn't afraid of work. If you have had specifically related job experience, this should of course be emphasized. However, if you have had no job history, you should omit this section completely.

Organizations and Awards will show your prospective employer that you are a well-rounded person with many interests. If you have had any position of leadership, you should include it, as it will indicate to a prospective employer that you have executive ability. Employers normally react favorably to religious work, such as teaching Sunday school. A religious person is generally viewed as more mature and stable.

Personal Data is not necessary. If included, the information should not appear negative. As an example, if you were 5'6" and weighed 220 pounds you would not want to include this.

References, although required by many employers after being hired as part of a formal job application, should not be submitted with résumés, nor should "To Whom It May Concern" letters of recommendation be attached. Any employer knows your references are going to be positive, or you wouldn't list them.

Your résumé should contain no negative data. The purpose of the résumé is to give just enough information to interest a particular firm to the point that they will want to investigate you further. It's really like a short advertisement to get the buyer to inspect the product.

If you are interested in several career areas, you should consider several different résumés, each aimed directly at a specific career field. Keep in mind that employers are not interested in employees for just any job; they are interested in specific areas.

During your interview you should not ask questions about salary or fringe benefits. It might be naive on the part of employers, but they expect employees to be primarily interested in the work and not in the benefits. After you are accepted by the employer, of course, you should discuss wages.

If the employer asks you what you want in the line of salary, it is best to state that you would expect to be treated in a fair manner but that the job is of primary importance. If you state a salary too high, chances are you won't get a job offer, and if you state a salary too low, the employer might wonder why.

Keep in mind that in the long run, directly related work experience in your career area is worth far more than non-related work experience, even when it might be at a far greater salary.

For summer jobs outside your area, you will have to rely on the mails.

EMPLOYMENT LETTERS

If one of your professors will recommend you to an employer he knows, this can be extremely effective. By stating in your letter, "Professor Hubert Hodgekins of the Engineering School at State College suggested I write to you," you have opened the door; providing, of course, that the recipient holds Professor Hodgekins in high esteem.

You should not address a letter to Personnel Director, President, or just the firm name. This is much like your receiving a letter addressed to "Occupant."

By checking on the firms from the sources given, you should know the names of the presidents as well as particular managers. You should write directly to a named person as closely related to the person you would work for as possible.

While you wish to avoid personnel people at this stage of the job search, you do not want to alienate them. Therefore, a copy of the letter and résumé should be sent to the personnel department.

It is far more difficult to sell yourself on paper to a person who perhaps does not have a formal job opening than it is in person. Therefore, you need to spend time composing your letter and résumé. One example of a letter of introduction is shown in the box.

Donaldson Engineering
4725 Midway Boulevard
Adonburg, Ohio 58731

Attn: Mr. Henry Johnson, Director of Engineers

Dear Mr. Johnson:

I am extremely interested in the work you are doing in stress analysis. I was especially impressed by the article in the December issue of *Engineering Monthly.*

I am a freshman in the School of Engineering at State University and am very interested in obtaining a position for the summer with your firm. As you will see from my enclosed résumé, my educational goals and experience to date are directly related to your work.

I will call you Thursday, March 2, to see when it might be convenient to meet with you personally.

Yours truly,

This letter immediately shows Mr. Johnson that you know something about the firm and are interested in a particular summer job, not just any summer job.

By letting him know that you will call him, Mr. Johnson is forced to think about whether he can use you. If, when you call, you are able to get an interview, chances are they are seriously considering hiring you. Generally, a firm will not have someone come any distance for an interview, especially for only a summer position, unless they expect to be hiring.

Of course, if you are unable to get an interview when you call, all it has cost you is a phone call. (Never call collect when inquiring for a job, as this will really turn people off.)

If you cannot afford to travel a great distance for a summer job interview, and even long-distance phone calls will seriously impair your budget, then a simple last sentence, such as the following, would be appropriate: "I am looking forward to hearing from you."

COLLEGE RECRUITING

Before you graduate, chances are there will be many college recruiters from various industries coming to your campus. Generally, either the guidance or student employment office will post notices of these interviews. If you are interested in any of the firms, you should sign up for an interview. Before any interview you should learn all you can about the firm. Besides the sources previously mentioned, you can write for a copy of the annual stockholders' report. Recruiters complain that most college students coming to interviews don't have the slightest idea of what the firm they are being interviewed by really does. By proper research, you can increase your competitive chances considerably.

Since these college interviewers often ask you to fill out a formal employment application, you should be sure to have your social security number, names and addresses of former employers and supervisors, and names and addresses of at least three references. References should be people to whom your interviewer can relate, such as people in the same general field or professors in your major field of study.

Sometimes college recruiters have the power to hire on the spot. More often, if they are interested, they will pay your expenses for a trip to their headquarters, where you will have a first-hand opportunity to see what the firm does. The visit will give the employer a chance to learn about you, and you will have the opportunity to learn about the employer.

You might have a series of interviews. The personnel department would be interested in your personal adjustment and the prospects of your continued career growth. The people you would be working for, or with, are interested in what kind of a fellow worker you would make and what you really know from your education and past experience.

These interviews are a two-way street. You must convince the employer you are the right person for the position, and the employer must convince you that the job is the right job for you. Both employer and prospective employee must be satisfied.

If you receive a job offer and are not sure about whether or not you should accept, ask for some time to consider it. A job is a big decision, and an employer will normally give you time for acceptance or rejection.

All too often graduates accept the first job offer they get, or else the one that offers the most money, without really analyzing whether the job is one they will be happy with. While no job is going to be ideal in every aspect, and some trade-offs may be necessary as to what you want, the job you accept must fulfill your priority needs.

Besides waiting for recruiters to come to your school, there is a great deal that you can be doing during your senior year for your career job search.

Since firms cannot visit every school, especially many smaller colleges, they simply send letters to the schools stating their employment needs. Your school's student employment office will have this information and sometimes applications to be submitted. If the employer is interested, he will contact you.

If there are other schools in the area, find out which employers are visiting them. Generally there will be no problem in utilizing their services.

SOURCES FOR JOB IDEAS

Professional and trade publications list many positions, as does the *Wall Street Journal.* Your school library probably has newspapers from other areas. You can also check newsstands for out-of-town papers or order the Sunday edition, with the large want-ad section, direct from the publisher.

Besides the want-ads you can obtain many employment leads from feature and news articles. Clues to jobs will be retirements, promotions, building permits, new leases, relocations, new products, etc. All of these, and many more, indicate that people will be hired.

You should also consider placing an ad in a professional journal dealing with your career area. This is especially helpful if you are looking for a highly specialized position.

Other people can help you find a position. Check with your instructors, current and past; they generally have many students already employed at various levels in firms in your career area. If they can help, they will. Your Christmas card list shows your friends. Each of your friends knows many people. You should recruit your friends to help you look for the type of job you are seeking. People you pay money to, such as your insurance agent and your banker, can be very helpful.

Your religious leader knows many people and should not be overlooked. Even high school instructors, especially in your general field, can be helpful. You should not expect anyone else to obtain a job for you, but it helps to have as many people as possible aware that you are seeking a particular type of position. A great number of jobs are filled without even being advertised because someone knows someone who is interested in that particular type of work.

You should consider taking the Professional and Administrative Career Examination (PACE) during your senior year. This is the entry level examination for federal employment and gets you on the Civil Service Register. Uncle Sam is our largest employer and has positions in every imaginable discipline. When you get on the Civil Service Register, you should send Standard Form 171 (employment application) to each government agency which you feel could use your training. Besides sending the forms to the agency in Washington, D.C., you can also send them to each of their regional offices.

You should not limit your career job search to vacancies only. Many firms create vacancies for the right applicant. Others keep the application on file until a vacancy appears.

Some private employment services are very worthwhile, especially those specializing in a particular career area. They usually have fees equal to one month's earnings. Often the employer will pay part or all of this fee. You should read any contract you sign carefully, as some firms have clauses making them your exclusive representative and, therefore, obligating you to a fee no matter how you obtain a position.

Avoid advance-fee career consultants. Generally, these firms are "ripoffs" and offer very little for a large fee. State employment agencies are usually worthless for college graduates. Generally, people contacting them are looking for cheap labor.

Contacting executive recruiters is also a waste of time. These recruiters have few specific jobs to be filled and are looking for people with a great deal of experience for these positions. They do not look for jobs to fit people. Because of this, it would be sheer luck for your qualifications to come across a recruiter's desk at the same time there was an opening requiring your qualifications.

Avoid having your résumé prepared by résumé shops. "Canned" résumés usually are so general that they are discarded. You should prepare your own personal résumé, tailored to specific jobs. This may mean a change in emphasis on a résumé for a slightly different position.

Writing letters and résumés and making phone calls will keep you busy. Finding the right job isn't always easy, and the more specialized the job, generally the longer it is going to take you.

You should use the basic techniques covered for writing résumés and letters. For experience, show only applicable work experience. If this is lacking, then list courses you have taken that are directly related to the job you are seeking.

INTERVIEWS AFTER GRADUATION

For your job interviews, you should be prepared for the following:

1. A question which allows you to tell about yourself. Be organized and give data that fit in with the needs of the position being applied for.
2. A question about why you wish to work for the firm. You should be able to show how your goals coincide with the firm's goals.
3. A question about your future aspirations. Your future goals should be progressive, along the same line as the position you are applying for. If not, you are probably applying for the wrong job.
4. A chance to ask questions. This gives you an excellent opportunity to show the depth of your knowledge concerning the employer.
5. Questions about social adjustment. Professional interviewers will ask questions designed to determine whether you have any social problems and to reveal the type of person you are in terms of your attitudes and values.

For further information about writing résumés and letters, as well as specific questions that you can expect in an interview, I recommend my *Work Experience Handbook,* published by Canfield Press.

Over one million jobs are filled every month in the United States. You can find a job; more importantly, you can find a job that meets your individual needs.

NOTES

Appendix A

Your College Information

Fill in the following checklist for a ready reference of important information about your school and community services.

Activities card (where to obtain): _____

_____

_____

Advisor

    My faculty advisor is: _____

    Office location: _____ Phone: _____

    Office hours are: _____

Alcohol (campus rules regarding alcoholic beverages): _____

_____

_____

Athletics

    For information on intramural athletics: _____

_____

_____

    For information on intercollegiate athletics: _____

_____

_____

Attendance (rules about being dropped): _____

_____

_____

_____

Audiovisual center (location): _____

_____

_____

Banking

    Location:_____

    Hours:_____

Behavioral problems (information on suspension and expulsion):_____

_____

_____

_____

Birth control information available at:_____

_____

_____

_____ Phone:_____

Book store

    Location:_____

_____

    Hours:_____

Bulletin boards (posting information):_____

_____

_____

Bursar's office (location): _____

_____

_____ Phone: _____

Carpool information:_____

_____

_____

Catalog (copies available at):_____

_____

Check cashing

    Checks may be cashed at:_____

_____

    Hours:_____

Child care center:_____

_____

_____

Clubs and organizations

Name of Clubs	Person to Contact
_____	_____
_____	_____
_____	_____
_____	_____
_____	_____
_____	_____
_____	_____
_____	_____
_____	_____
_____	_____
_____	_____

Copy center:
    Location:_____
    Phone: _____
  Individual copier
    Location:_____
    Cost: _____

Counselor
    My counselor is:_____
    Office location:_____ Phone: _____
        (Note: your advisor is a regular teacher, but your counselor is
        a professional trained to help you on career, curriculum, and
        personal problems.)

Counseling
    Educational and career counseling available at:_____
_____
_____ Phone:_____
    Personal counseling available at:_____
_____ Phone:_____

Crisis
    For serious problems such as suicide prevention or drugs or alcohol
    problems, contact:_____
_____
_____
_____
_____

Dean of Instruction:_____
    Office: _____ Phone:_____

Dean of Students:_____
    Office:_____ Phone:_____

Drug counseling and information
    Location:_____

_____
_____ Phone:_____

Educational opportunity program
    Location:_____

_____
_____ Phone:_____

Employment service
    Campus employment office: _____
_____ Phone:_____
    Community **employment office:** _____
_____ Phone:_____

Equal opportunity
    For problems involving discrimination, contact:_____

_____
_____
_____

Field studies programs:
    Information about off-campus study programs available from_____

_____

Financial aid office
    Location:_____

_____
_____ Phone:_____

Food service
    Location:_____

_____
_____ Hours:_____

Grades (where and when sent):_____
_____
_____

Grade points
     The school is on a _____ point system. An A is considered _____
     points, a B _____ points, a C _____ points and a D_____ points.
     Grade point average is computed by: _____
_____
_____
_____
_____

Graduate school information (where available): _____
_____
_____
_____
_____

Handicapped services:_____
_____
_____
_____

Health services:
     Student health office is located at: _____
_____ Phone:_____
     Hours:_____
     Additional information:_____
_____

Housing office
   Information for on-campus housing
     Location:_____ Phone: _____
   Information for off-campus housing
     Location: _____
_____ Phone:_____

Instructors' office hours
   Name of Instructor   Office Location   Office Hours
   _____   _____   _____
   _____   _____   _____
   _____   _____   _____
   _____   _____   _____
   _____   _____   _____
   _____   _____   _____
   _____   _____   _____

Insurance information (student health, life, and accident):_____

_____

_____

_____

_____

_____

_____

Laundry facilities
    Location:_____

_____

    Hours: _____

Legal aid
    Location: _____

_____

    Hours:_____
    Phone for appointment:_____

Library
    Campus location:_____

_____

    Hours:_____
    Late book charges:_____

_____

    Community location:_____

_____

    Hours:_____
    Late book charges: _____

Lost and found office (location):_____
_____ Phone:_____

Mail:_____

_____

Maintenance office (location):_____
_____ Phone:_____

Maps
    Campus maps may be obtained at:_____
    Community maps may be obtained at:_____

_____

Mathematics laboratory:_____

_____

_____

Messages: _____

_____

_____

Newspaper: _____

_____

Notary public: _____

_____

Parking information:_____

_____

_____

Police
  Campus location: _____

_____

    Campus phone:_____
  Community location:_____
    Phone:_____
Press releases:_____

_____

_____

Probation information and restrictions: _____

_____

_____

_____

Reading laboratory:_____

_____

_____

Rooms (reservations for campus activities): _____
_____
_____

R.O.T.C. location: _____
_____ Phone: _____

Registration office: _____
_____ Phone: _____

Scholarship information: _____
_____
_____
_____
_____

Schedule of classes: _____
_____
_____
_____
_____

School activities
    Information will be available at: _____
_____
_____
_____

Smoking regulations: _____
_____
_____

Social Security benefit information: _____
_____
_____

Student government office: _____
_____
_____ Phone: _____

Telephones
    Use of campus phones: _____
_____

Pay phones are located:_____
_____
_____

Television course information:_____
_____
_____
_____
_____
_____

Tickets
    Tickets for campus-held events will be available at:_____
_____
_____
_____

Transcripts (available at): _____
_____
_____Charge: _____
Tutorial program:_____
_____
_____
_____
_____

Typewriters (available for students): _____
_____
_____ Hours:_____

Veterans' office:_____
_____ Phone:_____

Welfare assistance information: _____
_____
_____
_____

Withdrawal procedure: _____
_____
_____
_____

Work experience education:_____
_____
   Office location:_____
_____ Phone:_____
Women's center:_____
_____
_____
_____

Writing laboratory: _____
_____
_____
_____
_____

Appendix B

Basic Drug Information

Alcohol. It may seem strange to list alcohol as a drug, but drinking is a major college drug problem. Addiction to alcohol is a serious illness, for which the only cure is total abstinence.

Liquor is the social lubricant of our society. It makes people feel relaxed and generally uninhibited. Unlike the other drugs described in this section, drinking is an acceptable and even condoned social activity, and alcoholics can usually delude themselves and others about the seriousness of their addiction.

Alcoholism causes damage to the brain, liver, and blood vessels. If you think you are becoming a problem drinker, talk to your counselor; don't be afraid to seek help.

Amphetamines. Because of their stimulant effect, these drugs are collectively known as "speed." Among their effects, amphetamines stimulate the nervous system, depress appetite, and diminish fatigue (hence their popularity at exam time). As the effects of the drug wear off, the speed user experiences fatigue and depression.

Amphetamines have not been proved to be addictive, but their damaging effects to body and mind are beyond question. It is true that "Speed kills."

Barbiturates. These drugs are usually prescribed for insomnia. Among the common brand names are Quaalude, Nembutal, and Seconal. In addition to making you sleepy, barbiturates can cause a feeling of euphoria, depression, and confusion or loss of memory. They are addictive, and withdrawal can be very difficult.

Cocaine. Because of its cost, cocaine (or "coke") is generally considered a rich person's drug. You may have heard that cocaine is safe to use because it is not addictive. Bear in mind, however, that many drugs are psychologically addictive.

Unlike heroin, which slows down body processes, cocaine is a stimulant. The high that it provides is often followed by depression and a slowing of the heartbeat, which can be dangerous. Although it can be injected, cocaine usually is sniffed, and continual inhalation can damage the nasal passages.

Glue sniffing.   Inhaling the fumes of various flammables such as glue, gasoline, or nail polish is probably the most foolish and most dangerous of drug-related activities.

The fumes, which are usually sniffed from a plastic bag, produce intoxication. Sniffing can also result in liver damage, major brain damage, convulsions, and death. Inhalation of flammable fumes from aerosol containers frequently results in sudden death.

Marijuana.   Smoking of the dried leaves and flowers of the weed *Cannabis sativa* produces feelings of euphoria. Large doses can cause hallucinations and LSD-type experiences. Marijuana goes by many names, including grass, pot, tea, and maryjane. It can be smoked, eaten, or made into tea. It is not believed to be physically addictive, but psychological dependency can occur.

Opiates.   These derivatives of the opium poppy are depressants. The most common form, heroin, is a white, off-white, or brown powder known by many street names, such as "horse," "smack," or "junk." (Other opium derivatives include morphine and codeine.) Heroin can be taken orally or inhaled, although it is usually melted over a flame into a solution and injected into a vein. It causes a feeling of euphoria. The pupils dilate, and the user is likely to fall asleep. Sensory perceptions and hunger, sex, and aggressive drives are reduced.

Heroin is addictive. People become addicted at different rates, but about 20 per cent of those who experiment with heroin become addicted. Addicts suffer a number of physical and mental disorders. Loss of appetite can lead to malnutrition, and use of unsterilized needles can result in hepatitis. After a period of use, the original dose no longer provides a feeling of euphoria, and a greater amount of the drug is needed to obtain the desired results. Thus the addiction becomes increasingly expensive, and sometimes users resort to crime to support their habit.

Attempts at withdrawal result in cramps, chills, and pain. Only a small portion of addicts are ever able to permanently kick the habit. If you are searching for a new experience, heroin isn't one of the better choices you could make.

Psychedelics and hallucinogens.   The most well known of these "trip" drugs is LSD. Others in this category include mescaline, peyote, and psilocybin. These drugs, which are highly unpredictable in effect, often cause the user to perceive things that are not objectively present (hallucinate) and may result in extremes of euphoria or depression. They are not addictive, but much remains to be learned about their effects on the body.

Appendix C

Bibliography

CHAPTER 1   SELF ANALYSIS

A Career Workbook for Liberal Arts Students
    Howard E. Figler
    Cranston, R.I., The Carroll Press, 1975
Careers: An Overview
    Robert M. Worthington
    Englewood Cliffs, N.J., Prentice-Hall, Inc., 1977
Career Decision
    D. K. Byrn
    Washington, D.C., National Vocational Guidance Association, 1969
Career Development for the College Student
    Philip W. Dunphy (ed.)
    Cranston, R.I., The Carroll Press, 1973
Career Explanation and Planning
    Bruce E. Shertzer
    Boston, Houghton Mifflin Co., 1973
Career Information Kit
    Chicago, Science Research Associates, Inc.
Career Opportunities: Community Services & Related Specialists
    Sylvia Bayliss et al. (eds.)
    Garden City, N.Y., Doubleday, 1970
Career Opportunities—Marketing, Business, & Office Specialists
    Garland D. Wiggs (ed.)
    Garden City, N.Y., Doubleday, 1973
Career Perspective, Your Choice of Work
    Celia Denues
    Worthington, Ohio, Charles A. Jones Publishing Co., 1972
College Guide for Jewish Youth
    Washington, D.C., B'nai B'rith Career and Counseling Service
Concise Handbook of Occupations
    Chicago, J. G. Ferguson Publishing Co.
Desk Top Career Kit
    Largo, Fla., Careers, Inc.

Dictionary of Occupational Titles
    Washington, D.C., U.S. Department of Labor, Bureau of Employment Security
Encyclopedia of Associations, 10th ed.
    Margaret Fisk and Mary W. Pair (eds.)
    Vol. 1: National Organizations of the United States
    Vol. 2: Geographic-Executive Index
    Detroit, Gale Research Co., 1973
Encyclopedia of Business Information Sources, 3rd ed.
    Paul Wasserman (ed.)
    Detroit, Gale Research Company, 1976
Encyclopedia of Careers and Vocational Guidance
    William E. Hopke (ed.)
    Vol. I: Planning Your Career
    Vol. II: Careers and Occupations
    Garden City, N.Y., Doubleday, 1975
Guide to Careers Through Vocational Training
    Edwin Whitfield and Richard Hoover
    N.Y., Robert R. Knapp, 1968
I Can Be Anything, Careers and Colleges for Young Women
    Joyce Slayton Mitchell
    New York, College Entrance Examination Board, 1975
If You Really Knew Me, Would You Still Like Me
    Eugene Kennedy
    Chicago, Argus Communications, 1975
Life Career Game
    S. S. Boocock
    Indianapolis, Ind., The Bobbs-Merrill Company, Inc.
Man in a World at Work
    H. Borow
    Boston, Houghton Mifflin Co., 1964
Modern Vocational Trends Reference Handbook
    J. Angel
    New York, World Trade Academy Press, 1963
Non-Traditional Careers for Women
    Sarah Splaver
    New York, Julian Messner, 1973
Occupational Information
    Robert Hoppock
    New York, McGraw-Hill Book Co., 1976
Occupational Information
    M. F. Baer and E. C. Roeber
    Chicago, Science Research Associates, Inc., 1958
Occupational Outlook Handbook
    Washington, D.C., U.S. Department of Labor, Bureau of Labor Statistics
Paraprofessionals: Careers of the Future and the Present
    Sarah Splaver
    New York, Julian Messner, 1972

Study of Values
    Allport, Vernon and Lindzey
    Boston, Houghton Mifflin Co., 1960
The Book: On the Taboo Against Knowing Who You Are
    Alan Watts
    N.Y., Vintage Books, 1972
The Psychology of Careers
    Donald Super
    New York, Harper & Row, 1957
The Psychology of Occupations
    Anne Roe
    New York, John Wiley & Sons, 1966
Where Do I Go from Here With My Life
    John C. Crystal and Richard N. Bolles
    New York, The Seabury Press, 1947
Work Experience Handbook
    William H. Pivar
    San Francisco, Canfield Press, 1976

CHAPTER 2   GOAL SETTING

Work Experience Handbook
    William H. Pivar
    San Francisco, Canfield Press, 1976

CHAPTER 3   PREPARING YOURSELF FOR SUCCESS

Beyond Success and Failure: Ways to Self-Reliance and Maturity
    Willard and Marguerite Beecher
    New York, The Julian Press, Inc., 1966
I'm O.K., You're A Pain In The Neck
    Albert Vorspan
    Garden City, N.Y., Doubleday, 1976
Improving Yourself
    Gary Yanker and Jack White
    New York, Dodd, 1975
Positive Addiction
    William Glasser
    New York, Harper & Row, 1976
Psycho-Cybernetics
    Maxwell Maltz
    Englewood Cliffs, N.J., Prentice-Hall, Inc., 1960
Self Therapy: Techniques for Personal Growth
    Muriel Schiffman
    Menlo Park, CA., Schiffman, 1967

The Power of Positive Thinking
    Norman Vincent Peale
    Englewood Cliffs, N.J., Prentice-Hall, Inc., 1952
The You That Could Be
    Fitzhugh Dodson
    Chicago, Follett Publishing Co., 1976
This is Earl Nightingale
    Earl Nightingale
    Garden City, N.Y., Doubleday, 1969
Your Erroneous Zones
    Wayne W. Dyer
    New York, Funk & Wagnall, 1976

CHAPTER 4   PLANNING YOUR CURRICULUM

Barron's Profile of American Colleges
    Benjamin Fine
    N.Y., Barron, 1973
Choosing a College: The Test of a Person
    John C. How
    New York, Delacorte Press, 1967
College Ahead: A Guide for High School Students and Their Parents
    Eugene S. Wilson and Charles A. Bucher
    New York, Harcourt Brace Jovanovich, 1973
Guide to College Majors
    Chronicle Guidance Research Department
    Moravia, N.Y., Chronicle Guidance Publications, 1973
Guide to the Evaluation of Educational Experiences in the Armed Forces
    Washington, D.C., American Council on Education.
How to Plan for College
    Frank S. Endicott
    Chicago, Rand McNally & Company, 1967
How to Prepare for College
    Abraham Lass
    New York, Washington Square Press, 1964
Lovejoy's College Guide, 13th ed.
    Clarence E. Lovejoy
    New York, Simon & Schuster, 1976
Planning for College
    Sidney Margolius
    New York, Avon Books, 1965
The Guide to College Life
    Joyce Slayton Mitchell
    Englewood Cliffs, N.J., Prentice-Hall, Inc., 1968
The Overeducated American
    Richard Freeman
    New York, Academic Press, 1976

The New York Times Guide to College Selection
    Ella Mazel
    New York, Quadrangle Books, 1972

CHAPTER 5   HOW TO STUDY

A Guide to College Survival
    William F. Brown and Wayne H. Holtzman
    Englewood Cliffs, N.J., Prentice-Hall, Inc., 1972
A Student's Guide to Efficient Study
    D. E. James
    Elmsford, N.Y., Pergamon Press, 1967
Better Reading Book
    Elizabeth Simpson
    Chicago, Science Research Associates, Inc., 1962
Effective Reading
    Francis P. Robinson
    New York, Harper & Row, 1962
Effective Study
    Francis P. Robinson
    New York, Harper & Row, 1946
Efficient Reading
    James I. Brown
    Indianapolis, Heath & Company, 1962
Homework
    Grace R. Langdon and Irving W. Stout
    New York, Day, 1969
How to Become a Better Reader
    Paul Witty
    Chicago, Science Research Associates, Inc., 1953
How to Study
    Ralph C. Preston and Morton Botel
    Chicago, Science Research Associates, Inc., 1956
How to Study
    Thomas F. Staton
    New York, McQuiddy Printing Co., 1962
How to Study Better and Get Higher Marks
    Eugene H. Ehrlich
    New York, Thomas Y. Crowell Co., 1962
How to Study in College
    Walter Pauk
    Boston, Houghton Mifflin Co., 1962
I Wish I'd Known That Before I Went to College
    Judy Brown and Donald Grossfield
    New York, An Essandess Special Edition, 1966

Improving College Reading
    Lee A. Jacobus
    New York, Harcourt, Brace & World, 1967
Improving Reading Skills in College Subjects
    Marie R. Cherinton
    New York, Teachers College Press, 1961
Learning to Study
    William W. Farquhar, John D. Krumboltz, and C. Gilbert Wrenn
    New York, Ronald Press Co., 1960
Purposeful Reading in College
    James M. McCallister
    New York, Appleton-Century-Crofts, 1942
Reading Skills
    William D. Baker
    Englewood Cliffs, N.J., Prentice-Hall, Inc., 1953
Study Is Hard Work
    William H. Armstrong
    New York, Harper & Row, 1956
Study Skills: A Student's Guide for Survival
    Robert A. Carman and Royce Adams, Jr.
    New York, John Wiley & Sons, 1972
The Adventure of Learning in College
    Roger H. Garrison
    New York, Harper & Row, 1954

CHAPTER 6   HOW TO TAKE AN EXAMINATION

How to Study and Take Exams
    Lincoln Pettit
    New York, J. F. Rider, 1960
Score: The Strategy of Taking Tests
    Darrell Huff
    New York, Appleton-Century-Crofts, 1961

CHAPTER 7   HOW TO WRITE A TERM PAPER

A Manual for the Writers of Term Papers, Theses and Dissertations, 4th ed.
    Kate L. Turabian
    Chicago, University of Chicago Press, 1973
A Reading Approach to College Writing
    Martha Cox
    Scranton, Pa., Chandler Publishing Co., 1971
A Research Manual for College Studies and Papers
    Cecil B. Williams
    New York, Harper & Row, 1951

Anatomy of a Theme
   Robert H. Meyer
   Beverly Hills, Ca., Glencoe Press, 1969

Books, Libraries and You: A Handbook on the Use of Reference Books and the Reference Resources of the Library, 3rd ed.
   Jessie Boyd et al.
   New York, Charles Scribner's Sons, 1965

Elements of College Writing and Reading
   P. Joseph Canovar
   New York, McGraw-Hill Book Co., 1971

Guide to The Use of Books and Libraries
   Jean Gates
   New York, McGraw-Hill Book Co., 1962

Handbook For Pratical Composition
   Morriss H. Needleman
   New York, McGraw-Hill Book Co., 1968

How and Where to Look It Up
   New York, McGraw-Hill Book Co., 1958

Ideas and Patterns for Writing
   Carle B. Spotts
   New York, Holt, Rinehart and Winston, Inc., 1971

Reading, Writing, & Rhetoric, 3rd ed.
   James B. Hogins and Robert E. Yarber
   Chicago, Science Research Associates, 1975

Say It with Words
   Charles W. Ferguson
   Lincoln, University of Nebraska Press, 1954

The Experience of Writing
   William D. Baker and T. Benson Strandness
   Englewood Cliffs, N.J., Prentice-Hall, Inc., 1970

The Modern Researcher
   Jacques Barzun and Henry Graft
   New York, Harcourt, Brace & Co., 1957

The Research Paper: Gathering Library Material, Organizing and Preparing the Manuscript
   Lucyle Hooks
   Englewood Cliffs, N.J., Prentice-Hall, Inc., 1962

The Use of Books and Libraries
   Minnesota University Library School
   Minneapolis, University of Minnesota Press, 1958

The Writer's Voice: Dramatic Situations for College Writing
   Ken L. Symes
   New York, Holt, Rinehart and Winston, Inc., 1973

Using Books and Libraries
   Ella Aldrich
   Englewood Cliffs, N.J., Prentice-Hall, Inc., 1960

Writing a Technical Paper
    Donald H. Menzel and Howard M. Jones
    New York, McGraw-Hill Book Co., 1961
Writing: Process and Product
    Susan Miller
    Cambridge, Mass., Winthrop Publishers, Inc., 1976
Writing Without Teachers
    Peter Elbow
    New York, Oxford University Press, 1973

CHAPTER 8   FINANCING YOUR EDUCATION

A Parent's Guide to College Planning
    Frank S. Endicott
    New York, Rand McNally & Company, 1967
Anyone Can Get into College
    Herbert B. Livesey
    New York, Viking, 1971
Borrowing for College: A Guide for Students and Parents
    Washington, D.C., United States Office of Education
College Scholarship Guide
    Clarence E. Lovejoy and Theodore Jones
    New York, Simon and Schuster
Complete Planning for College: The Kiplinger Guide to Your Education Beyond
High School
    New York, McGraw-Hill Book Co., 1962
Financial Assistance for College Students: Undergraduates
    Washington, D.C., United States Office of Education
Going Right On
    Princeton, N.J., College Entrance Examination Board
How About College Financing? A Guide for Parents and College-Bound Students
    Norman S. Feingold
    Washington, D.C., American School Counselor Association
How to Beat the High Cost of College
    Claire Cox
    New York, Dial Press, 1971
How to Get Money for College
    Benjamin Fine and Sidney Eisenberg
    New York, Doubleday, 1964
I Wish I'd Known That Before I Went to College
    Judy Brown and Donald Grossfield
    New York, An Essandess Special Edition, 1966
Need A Lift
    Indianapolis, American Legion Education and Scholarship Program, American-
    ism and Children and Youth Division
Planning For College
    Sidney Margolius
    New York, Avon Books, 1965

Student Financial Help: A Guide to Money for College
    Louis T. and Joyce W. Scaring
    Garden City, N.Y., Doubleday, 1974
Your College Education: How to Pay for It
    Sarah Splaver
    New York, Julian Messner, Inc. 1964

CHAPTER 9   ADJUSTMENT TO THE COLLEGE ENVIRONMENT

A Guide to College Survival
    William F. Brown and Wayne H. Holtzman
    Englewood Cliffs, N.J., Prentice-Hall, Inc., 1972
Beyond Success and Failure: Ways to Self-Reliance and Maturity
    Willard and Marguerite Beecher
    New York, The Julian Press, 1966
Getting the Most Out of College
    Margaret Bennett, Molly Lewin, and Dorothy McKay
    New York, McGraw-Hill Book Co., 1957
How to Do a University
    Andrew Barclay, William Crano, Charles Thornton, and Arnold Werner
    New York, John Wiley & Sons, Inc., 1971
How to Talk with People
    Irving J. Lee
    New York, Harper & Row, 1952
I Wish I'd Known That Before I Went to College
    Judy Brown and Donald Grossfield
    New York, An Essandess Special Edition, 1966
Introduction to College
    Bert D. Anderson
    New York, Holt, Rinehart and Winston, Inc., 1969
Love and Sex in Plain Language
    Eric W. Johnson
    Philadelphia, J. B. Lippincott Co., 1965
Love and the Facts of Life
    Evelyn M. Duvall
    New York, Association Press, 1963
Love, Sex and the Teenager
    Rhoda Lorand
    Riverside, N.J., The Macmillan Company, 1965
Mastering the College Challenge
    Bette Soldwedel
    Riverside, N.J., The Macmillan Company, 1964
Motivation and Personality
    Abraham Maslow
    New York, Harper & Row, 1954
On Becoming an Educated Person
    Virginia Voeks
    Philadelphia, W. B. Saunders Company, 1957

Psychology of Personal and Social Adjustment
    Henry Clay Lindgren
    New York, American Book Company, 1959
The Art and Skill of Getting Along with People
    Sylvanus M. Duvall
    Englewood Cliffs, N.J., Prentice-Hall, Inc., 1961
The College Drug Scene
    James T. Carey
    Englewood Cliffs, N.J., Prentice-Hall, Inc., 1968
The College Scene: Students Tell It Like It Is
    James A. Foley and Robert K. Foley
    New York, Cowles, 1969
The Psychology of College Success; A Dynamic Approach
    Henry Clay Lindren
    New York, American Book Co., 1969
What About Teen-age Marriage
    Jeanne Sakol
    New York, Julian Messner, 1961

CHAPTER 10   EMPLOYMENT DURING AND AFTER COLLEGE

Dun & Bradstreet Directories
    N.Y., Dun & Bradstreet
Encyclopedia of Associations, 10th ed.
    Margaret Fisk and Mary W. Pair (eds.)
    Detroit, Gale Research Company, 1976
Encyclopedia of Business Information Sources, 3rd ed.
    Paul Wasserman (ed.)
    Detroit, Gale Research Company, 1976
Go Hire Yourself an Employer
    Richard Irish
    Garden City, N.Y., Anchor Books, 1973
Moody's Industrials
    N.Y., Moody's Investor Service Inc.
On-The-Job Training and Where to Get It
    Robert Liston
    New York, Julian Messner, 1973
Summer Employment Directory of the United States, 26th rev. ed.
    Mypena A. Leith
    Cincinnati, National Directory Service Inc., 1976
The National Directory of Employment Services
    Detroit, Gale Research Company
Thomas Register
    N.Y., Thomas Publishing Co.
Work Experience Handbook
    William H. Pivar
    San Francisco, Canfield Press, 1976

Index

True-false tests, guessing on, 67

Upper division course, definition of, 33

Venereal disease (VD), 108-109